D1622307

A Cup of Java

An Introduction to Programming

Second Edition

J. Denbigh Starkey
Montana State University

Kendall Hunt
publishing company

www.kendallhunt.com
Send all inquiries to:
4050 Westmark Drive
Dubuque, IA 52004-1840

Printed in the United States of America
10 9 8 7 6 5 4 3

This book is dedicated to our daughter

Lt. Susan Starkey
Helicopter Aircraft Commander, U.S. Navy

Your mother and I are very proud of your accomplishments

Table of Contents

Preface xi

Chapter 1. Introduction to Computers and Programming 1
  1.1 Programming 1
    1.1.1 Algorithms *vs.* Programs 2
    1.1.2 Why Java? 2
    1.1.3 The programming process 3
    1.1.4 Programming in the real world–working as a team 4
  1.2 The Computer 4
  1.3 What Happens When You Submit a Java Program? 7
  1.4 Computer Science 8
  1.5 Exercises 9
    General questions 9

Chapter 2. A First Java Program 11
  2.1 Introduction 11
  2.2 The Structure of a Class Definition 12
  2.3 The Class Header 13
  2.4 The Instance Fields 13
  2.5 Constructor Definition 15
  2.6 Method Declarations 16
  2.7 The Complete Class Definition 18
  2.8 Encapsulation 18
  2.9 A Summary of the Design Process Used in the Player Class Definition 19
  2.10 Exercises 20
    General questions 20
    In-lab programs 21
    Out-lab programs 22

Chapter 3. Implementing and Testing the Player Class under BlueJ 23
  3.1 Bringing up BlueJ 23
  3.2 Output Statements, System.out.print() and System.out.println() 29
    3.2.1 Method call notation 30
    3.2.2 System.out.println() 31
    3.2.3 System.out.print() 31
  3.3 Testing the Player Class with a UnitTest Class 32
  3.4 Unit Testing With JUnit 33
  3.5 Testing Strategies 37
  3.6 Exercises 38
    General questions 38
    In-lab programs 39
    Out-lab programs 39

Chapter 4. Debugging Your Program 41
  4.1 Introduction 41

4.2 Compile Errors **41**
4.3 Execution Errors **43**
    4.3.1 Infinite loops 43
    4.3.2 Abnormal termination (throwing an exception)............................. 43
    4.3.3 Normal termination with incorrect results 44
4.4 The BlueJ Debugger... **45**
4.5 Exercises **45**
    General questions.. 45
    In-lab programs 45
    Out-lab programs 45

Chapter 5. Variables and Their Definitions **47**
5.1 Introduction **47**
5.2 Declaring Variables **47**
    5.2.1 Commenting variable declarations 48
5.3 Legal and Appropriate Names for Variables, Methods, and Classes **48**
5.4 Primitive Data Types **49**
5.5 Scope of Variables... **52**
5.6 Exercises **53**
    General questions.. 53
    In-lab programs 55
    Out-lab programs 55

Chapter 6. Assignment Statements and Expressions **57**
6.1 Introduction **57**
6.2 Assignment Statements... **57**
6.3 Arithmetic Expressions **58**
    6.3.1 Arithmetic operators 59
    6.3.2 Operator precedence 61
    6.3.3 Increment and decrement operators (++ and --) 62
6.4 String Expressions **63**
6.5 Back to Assignment Statements... **64**
    6.5.1 Type casting.. 65
6.6 +=, -=, *=. /=, %= **66**
6.7 Assignment Statements with Objects **67**
6.8 Built-in Arithmetic Methods.. **68**
6.9 Built-in String Methods **69**
6.10 Accessor and Mutator Methods **70**
6.11 Exercises **71**
    General questions.. 71
    In-lab programs 72
    Out-lab programs 73

Chapter 7. Extending the Player Class..**75**
7.1 Introduction **75**
7.2 The Three New Classes.. **75**
    7.2.1 The JUnit Test class 75
    7.2.3 The Stats class.. 76

7.2.3 The New Player class 77
7.3 Instance Fields *vs.* Class Fields **78**
7.4 The Class Diagram **79**
7.5 Coupling **79**
7.6 Exercises **80**
General questions 80
In-lab programs 81
Out-lab programs 81

Chapter 8. Using Java's Online Documentation **83**
8.1 Introduction **83**
8.2 Why the Java Documentation Is Useful **83**
8.3 Using the Online Documentation **84**
8.4 Using Javadoc to Document Your Programs **89**
8.5 A Javadoc Example **89**
8.6 Exercises **90**
General questions 90
In-lab programs 91
Out-lab programs 91

Chapter 9. Conditional Statements **93**
9.1 Introduction **93**
9.2 The Simple if Statement **93**
9.3 Arithmetic Comparison Operators **95**
9.4 The if-then-else Statement **96**
9.5 A Common Mistake with boolean Valued Expressions **97**
9.6 Multiple Options: else-if Structures **98**
9.7 Multiple Options: The Switch Statement **99**
9.8 Comparing Floating Point Numbers for Equality **100**
9.9 Comparing Strings for Equality and Alphabetic Order **101**
9.10 Constants (final Declarations) **102**
9.11 The Selection Operator (Don't Use) **104**
9.12 boolean (Logical) Operators **105**
9.12.1 Precedence of boolean Operators 106
9.12.2 Short circuit evaluation of boolean expressions 106
9.13 Exercises **107**
General questions 107
In-lab programs 108
Out-lab programs 109

Chapter 10. Taking Control of Input/Output **111**
10.1 Introduction **111**
10.2 Structure of a format() Method Call **112**
10.2.1 Left and right justification of output values..................................... 114
10.3 System.out.printf() **114**
10.4 Other Uses for format() **115**
10.5 Reading Values from the Input Stream **115**
10.6 Instancing and Using a Scanner Object **115**

10.7 String Input..117
    10.7.1 nextline()...117
    10.7.2 next()...119
10.8 Dialog Boxes For Input...**119**
10.9 Dialog Boxes for Output...**120**
10.10 Example Program for I/O Dialog Boxes................................**121**
10.11 Exercises...**122**
    General questions...122
    In-lab programs 122
    Out-lab programs...123

Chapter 11. Looping Statements **125**
11.1 Introduction..**125**
11.2 Example: Summing the First _n_ Integers **125**
    11.2.1 Approach 1: The while loop..126
    11.2.2 Approach 2: The for statement.......................................127
    11.2.3 Approach 3: The do-while Statement..............................128
11.3 The for Statement...**128**
    11.3.1 Another for example 129
    11.3.2 Things to avoid 130
11.4 The while Statement...**130**
11.5 The do-while Statement..**131**
11.6 The foreach Statement (Preview) **132**
11.7 The BlueJ Debugger **132**
    11.7.1 The program to debug..133
    11.7.2 Setting a breakpoint..134
    11.7.3 Single step..135
    11.7.4 Step into...137
    11.7.5 Summary and debugging recommendation......................137
11.8 Exercises...**138**
    General questions...138
    In-lab programs 139
    Out-lab programs...140

Chapter 12. 1D Arrays...**143**
12.1 Introduction..**143**
12.2 Simple Arrays...**143**
12.3 An Array Example: Saving Primes **145**
12.4 Initializing 1D Arrays..**148**
12.5 The foreach Statement...**149**
12.6 Exercises...**150**
    General questions...150
    In-lab programs 151
    Out-lab programs...151

Chapter 13. Array Lists...**153**
13.1 Introduction..**153**
13.2 Array List Implementation Details...**153**

13.3 An Array List Example **155**
   13.3.1 Class StudentRecord 155
   13.3.2 Class StudentDB 156
   13.3.3 Class UnitTest 157
   13.3.4 Class program output 158
13.4 Converting from an Array List to a 1D Array **158**
13.5 Wrapping Primitive Types in Array Lists **159**
13.6 Exercises **160**
   General questions 160
   In-lab programs 161
   Out-lab programs 161

Chapter 14. Multi-Dimensional Arrays **163**
14.1 Introduction **163**
14.2 2D Arrays **163**
14.3 Nested Loops **165**
14.4 2D Array Notation and Accessing Row and Column Sizes **165**
14.5 2D Array Example **166**
14.6 Non-Rectangular Arrays **170**
14.7 3D and Higher Dimension Arrays **171**
14.8 Exercises **174**
   General questions 174
   In-lab Programs 175
   Out-lab Programs 175

Chapter 15. Recursive Methods **177**
15.1 Introduction **177**
15.2 A Recursive Example: Computing Factorials **177**
15.3 Tower of Hanoi: A Recursive Solution **178**
15.4 Rules for Defining A Recursive Method **182**
15.5 Recursive Loops **182**
15.6 Why Recursion Is Important to Programmers **183**
15.7 Recursively Analyzing an Array **184**
15.8 Exercises **186**
   General questions 186
   In-lab programs 187
   Out-lab programs 188

Chapter 16. Inheritance **189**
16.1 Introduction **189**
16.2 An Inheritance Example **189**
   16.2.1 The Person superclass 191
   16.2.2 The Sudent subclass 192
   16.2.3 The Professor subclass 193
   16.2.4 The OfficeStaff subclass 194
   16.2.5 Class diagram for the inheritance example 195
   16.2.6 UnitTest class for the inheritance example 196
16.3 Cohesion **197**

16.4 Summary **197**

16.5 Exercises...**198**

    General questions... 198

    In-lab programs 200

    Out-lab programs 200

Chapter 17. Interfaces, Polymorphism, and Packages............................**201**

17.1 Introduction **201**

17.2 Using an Interface Class...**202**

17.3 More Details on Interface and Implements Definitions **206**

17.4 Packages **207**

17.5 Exercises...**208**

    General questions... 208

    In-lab programs 209

    Out-lab programs 209

Chapter 18. Exceptions and Exception Handling.....................................**211**

18.1 Introduction **211**

18.2 Standard Exceptions...**213**

18.3 Catching Built-in Exceptions...**214**

    18.3.1 Clearing Out the Bad Value in the Input Buffer after an Exception 215

18.4 Explicitly Throwing a Built-in Exception...**215**

18.5 Rolling Your Own Exceptions **217**

18.6 Summary of Exception Handling...**218**

18.7 Exceptions *vs.* Errors **219**

18.8 Exercises...**219**

    General questions... 219

    In-lab programs 220

    Out-lab programs 220

Chapter 19. Reading from and Writing to External Files **221**

19.1 Introduction **221**

19.2 Reading from a File...**221**

19.3 Some Overhead Details...**222**

19.4 A File Input Example **222**

19.5 Reading from Files and Writing to Files **223**

19.6 Exercises...**225**

    General questions... 225

    In-lab programs 226

    Out-lab programs 226

Appendix A: Downloading BlueJ and the Java JDK.................................**227**

A.1 Installing BlueJ **227**

A.1 Installing the Java JDK...**227**

Index **229**

Preface

There are many books on Java, and so why have I written another? There were two major reasons; as a teacher I have had problems with all of the current Java texts, and wanted to write one that fit better with my own teaching style, and I wanted to write a book that would help students write significant Java programs faster.

Java is an example of an Object-Oriented Programming Language, which means that programs are designed not as a set of procedures that call on each other, but on how to deal with the objects that the program is going to manipulate. Objects are designed through classes, which contain information on the objects and define the methods that will be used to manipulate them. Most Java books now use an approach called *objects first*, which means that before introducing concepts like loops and conditional statements they first develop some simple programs that typically use objects that are already defined in Java. Like most Computer Science instructors I think that objects first is the best approach to take, but I take it somewhat deeper than most other books.

Throughout my career teaching programming, using many different introductory languages, I have always been convinced that the best way to learn to program is to look at examples of programs first, and then describe in more detail what is going on in the programs. So the first program that you will see will just consist of a single class, where I'll show how to create objects and manipulate them. This lets you get into writing your own classes immediately, and so you'll be writing Java programs much faster. This also means that you won't be discouraged by having to work through tiresome definitions before you get your hands dirty with Java code.

Another difference in this book is that I am recommending that you use a Java environment called BlueJ to run your programs. BlueJ can be downloaded free to all common computer systems (Windows, Mac, Linux, etc.) and is ideal for providing support while you learn to program. If you continue to program in Java, you are likely to later use other more powerful integrated development environments (IDEs) like Eclipse (www.Eclipse.org) or NetBeans (www.NetBeans.org), which are also open source environments that can be downloaded free, but they aren't good for beginning programmers because you have to spend too much time concentrating on learning the complex environments instead of learning how to program in Java. In September 2008 the BlueJ and NetBeans groups provided a plug-in for BlueJ that lets you cross-develop software under BlueJ and NetBeans and so this greatly simplifies the transition to NetBeans 6.1 for complex Java programs. So in this book

I'll be giving you instructions on how to download BlueJ and use it to develop and debug your programs.

This is a good time to express my appreciation for groups like the BlueJ, NetBeans, and Eclipse teams, who provide very high-quality open source software free to the computing community.

BlueJ is a joint development between the University of Kent in England and Deakin University in Australia, with support from Sun Microsystems (who also developed Java). It is used around the world with the interface available in about 20 languages.

Chapter 1. Introduction to Computers and Programming

I'll get you writing your first programs in Java as quickly as possible, but before you can do that you need to have a basic understanding of modern computers and what happens when you run a program on a computer. In this chapter I'll cover these topics and then in Chapter 2 I'll describe how to write your first Java programs..

1.1 Programming

Programming is the art and science of giving instructions to a computer that tell it how to solve a specific problem. The problem can be trivial, like computing the area of a circle when you know its radius, to very complex like playing chess at an expert level or controlling the return of the space shuttle.

Programming is an art because there is no correct way to write a program for any problem, but some solutions (programs) are clearly much better than others. Every programmer develops their own programming style, and some programmers produce much more beautiful programs than others. A good program has a number of important features like correctness, efficiency, and how easily it can be read and understood by others. Obviously correctness is important because any program that gives incorrect results isn't much use to anyone, and in some cases correctness is critical because lives depend on your program being correct[1] and in other cases the economic cost of a programming error can be extreme.[2] How well your program can be read and understood becomes important if someone else has to modify your program and you aren't around to explain how it works.

Programming is also a science because we can mathematically analyze a program to see how efficient it is, and determine which of two or more competing programs is the best from an efficiency standpoint. For example, say we want to sort a list of numbers into ascending order. Some common sorting programs take an amount of time that is proportional to the square of the number of numbers being sorted, while others take an amount of time that is proportional to the number of elements times its logarithm. If we want to sort a million elements, this becomes a critical

---

[1] For example, the computer-based Therac-25 radiation therapy system occasionally gave patients massive, and sometimes lethal, radiation overdoses over an 18-month period before the problem was detected.
[2] The Mars Climate Orbiter crashed because part of the programming team (from Lockheed) used imperial measures (e.g., feet) and part (from JPL) used metric measures (e.g., meters) and as a result the orbiter made a $250 million hole in the Mars surface. The Mars Polar Lander, which took off at the same time as the orbiter, was also lost, and this is also blamed on a software error.

difference because 1,000,000 squared is 1,000,000,000,000 while 1,000,000 times $\log_2(1,000,000)$ is only 20,000,000.

1.1.1 Algorithms *vs.* Programs

When programming you will first design and compare one or more algorithms, which are your designs for a solution to the problem that you want to solve. Then you will then decide which is the best of your algorithms and implement it in a particular programming language (e.g., Java). This is an important distinction- the algorithm is a design of a solution to the problem, which can then be implemented in one of many computer languages as a program and run on the computer.

1.1.2 Why Java?

In this book I'll be using the language Java, which is generally accepted as the best language for beginning programmers. There are many programming languages available, and if you continue into a subsequent career where you program (whether as a computer scientist, a computer engineer, a developer of business applications, or any other professional), you will become expert at many languages over your career. For example I started on a language (now long dead) called Mercury Autocode before I went to university, then learned Algol 60 (also dead, although it influenced most modern languages, including Java) and some extensible languages when I first went to graduate school. Since then I have used a large number of languages like Fortran (various versions), SNOBOL, PL/I, SESPOOL, Lisp, Perl (my favorite language), C, C++, Java, and so on. Altogether I've programmed extensively in at least 25 programming languages. So while you are likely to use many languages, Java will provide you with an understanding of programming that makes it easier to learn to program in these other languages.

The modern programming style is to program using objects, and to assign behavior to objects and classes of objects. This is called OOP (Object-Oriented Programming) and the design of algorithms in an object-oriented fashion is called OOD (Object-Oriented Design). A language like Java that supports OOP and OOD is called an OOL (Object-Oriented Language).

So my goal is to teach modern programming, which means OOP. The three most common languages that support OOP are Java, C++, and C#, and so the selection of an introductory language is mainly restricted to them. C++ is essentially an object-oriented patch put on top of C, and so its OO capabilities aren't very clean. C# is very similar to Java but is effectively restricted to one vendor's software environments (Microsoft). Java, on the other hand, was designed as an OOL and so it is a much cleaner environment in which to be introduced to OOP than C++, and it can also be run on all standard systems (Windows-based, Macs, Linux, etc.), which is why I, and the faculty at a significant majority of universities, believe that it is the best language to use when learning to program.

Another reason for selecting Java is that its error messages are very descriptive. If you are running your C or C++ program and something breaks, then you usually get a completely useless error message, whereas with Java you can hope to get some help to find where the problem was. It also has superb documentation, which makes it easy to find out how its features work.

As I discussed above, it is unlikely that this will be the only language that you have to learn. Many of you will later use C, C++, or C#. Fortunately commands in these languages are very similar, and so once you have learned Java it is very easy to pick up one of the others. For example in all four of these languages (Java, C, C++, and C#) if you want to find the sum of the squares of the first ten positive integers, you can write:

```
squareSum = 0;
for (int i = 1; i <= 10; i++)
{
    squareSum += i * i;
}
```

Don't worry about the details of this yet–you'll see lots of loops like this as the book progresses–the only point that I'm making here is that the four languages are very similar in their basic commands, so if you know one, it is relatively easy to learn one of the others.

There are, of course, places where Java and C++ are rather different, such as their approaches to input/output and to arrays, but still transitioning between the languages isn't difficult.

As the example above shows, throughout this book code segments will be in a fixed width font with background shading. When code and constants appear inline in text (e.g., if I want to discuss the line `squareSum += i * i;`) I'll use the fixed width font shown here.

1.1.3 The programming process

So what is the programming process? The first two steps, before you ever start to write the program, are to make sure that you understand the problem that you should be solving and then to decide how you want to solve it (i.e., designing algorithms for the problem and selecting the best one). The next step is to implement the algorithm as a Java program and submit it to the computer where it

3

will be translated by a program called a compiler and then executed (run). At this point you might think that you are done, but unfortunately your Java program will almost always contain errors.[3] So first you'll fix errors detected by the compiler while it interprets your program, and then once all those errors have been fixed you'll probably find that your program is giving incorrect results, and so you have to test it with different input values and make changes until it runs correctly for every different kind of input that you can think of.

1.1.4 Programming in the real world—working as a team

When you first start to program, you'll be writing small programs that can hopefully be completed by a single programmer, but once you start programming in a commercial environment, you'll usually be writing small parts of huge programs, which are developed and modified over many years. How to handle the many problems introduced when moving from individual programming to team programming is part of a field of Computer Science called Software Engineering.

1.2 The Computer

You shouldn't treat the computer as just a magical black box, but should have a basic understanding of its major pieces and what happens when you give it a Java program, which I'll cover in this section and Section 1.3.

The heart of every computer is its *Central Processing Unit*, which is always just called the *CPU* or the *processor*. This has the hardware to do all of the basic operations that it needs, such as adding two integers, multiplying two floating point numbers, or checking to see whether two words are in alphabetical order. I'll just consider a simple computer where the CPU looks at its current instruction, obeys it (called executing the instruction), and then moves on to the next instruction. To keep things under control, it has an internal clock, which can be considered as providing a tick on a regular basis, and most instructions that it executes can be done in one clock cycle. So on one clock tick it executes an instruction, then by the next tick it has completed that one and will execute the next instruction, and so on until the program is finished. These clock ticks happen very fast. For example, say that you buy a 2 GHz computer; this means that it does two billion clock ticks per second. Looking at this differently this means that in the time taken to execute (run)

---

[3] I've been programming for over 40 years, and every time that I submit a program I still expect it to run without problems first time. By now I should know better; as this never happens except for the simplest programs. However if I submit a new program tomorrow, I'll still expect it to work immediately, and once again I'll be disappointed.

4

one instruction and move on to the next, light has traveled about six inches. Light might sound fast at 186,000 mph, but in a billionth of a second (called a nanosecond) it only goes about one foot, so in computer terms light crawls.

To be able to move from instruction to instruction so quickly and to be able, for example, to retrieve the numbers that you want it to add and then save the result somewhere, your program and its data must be stored in very fast memory that is very close to the processor (like everything else, electronic communication is limited by the speed of light, and as we have seen light is very slow in the time scale that we are looking at). So the CPU has an attached memory called the Random Access Memory, usually just called the RAM or the memory.[4] In a modern machine this can be very large–for example, on my personal computer I have 3 GB of memory. What does this mean? To answer this I must first look at the smallest memory units, bits and bytes.

The smallest unit of memory is a bit, which is short for binary digit, and has a value of 0 or 1, and a byte is a group of eight bits. Since 2^8 is 256, this means that a byte can store any one of 256 individual characters. A byte is the smallest memory unit that you usually access, and is typically large enough to store a single character of information (e. g., the letter S, a space, the $ character, or whatever). So storing my name, Denbigh Starkey, in memory with one byte for each character will take 15 bytes. In Java characters like this will be assigned two bytes, and so my name will take 30 bytes of storage, which lets Java support much more varied character sets in many different languages. Numbers are stored efficiently and so most systems will store an integer like -321,654,987 in four bytes and a floating point number like π in four or eight bytes, depending on the processor and the programmer's choice.[5] Of course π is infinitely long[6] in its representation (3.141592...) and so it will be rounded after a while to fit into four or eight bytes.

The ways in which we usually describe computer memories and other storage range down from terabytes to bytes.[7] The meanings of the names are shown in the following table:

---

[4] It is still often called core memory, which dates back to the 50s and 60s when each bit (a binary digit, so 0 or 1) was stored as the magnetic orientation of a small donut-shaped ring of metal called a core. Each core had three wires running through it to make it possible to set and read the orientation, so even 1000 bits took up a lot of space.

[5] I'll be creating floating point numbers with the Java keyword double, which will assign eight bytes to each.

[6] Technically π is a real, not a floating point number, which means that it cannot be represented accurately with a finite number of digits.

[7] Larger external storages with petabyte (10^{15}) or even exabyte (10^{18}) sizes are now occasionally seen, but they aren't common yet.

Name	Shorthand	Approximate size	Actual size
Terabyte	TB	1 trillion (2^{40}, $\sim 10^{12}$) bytes	1,099,511,627,776 bytes
Gigabyte	GB	1 billion (2^{30}, $\sim 10^{9}$) bytes	1,073,741,824 bytes
Megabyte	MB	1 million (2^{20}, $\sim 10^{6}$) bytes	1,048,576 bytes
Kilobyte	K or KB	1 thousand (2^{10}, $\sim 10^{3}$) bytes	1024 bytes

As you can see, while it is easiest (and common) to refer to, say, a megabyte as 1 million bytes, it is actually slightly larger than that.[8] This all comes from memory hardware units coming in powers of 2, and 2^{10} is 1024, 2^{20} is 1,048,576, etc. So returning to my original question, my computer's 3 GB memory has about three billion bytes of storage.

Over the years memories have become far larger than they used to be because memory technology has become far cheaper. For example, the first computer that I programmed, which was the only computer at the Royal Aircraft Establishment (a large British government research and development lab where I worked for eight months before going to university) had 1K of memory, and so my personal PC now has 3 million times as much. This increase has changed how we program.

In addition to the RAM, computers also have a much smaller, and much faster (and hence, more expensive) memory called the *cache memory*. The CPU tries to copy the values and the instructions that it is likely to need next from the main memory into the cache so that it can access them faster. Any time that it needs to retrieve something from the RAM instead of the cache it typically misses one or more clock cycles while it waits. Cache memories are small relative to the RAM (e.g., my computer has two 4 MB cache memories), but very high cache hit rates (finding needed values in the cache) are achieved. For most applications you can expect cache hit rates (the percentage of values needed that are in the cache) to be in the high 90s. Hit rates of 98% are not unusual. Modern computers often have multiple caches (e.g., separate caches for instructions and data) and/or multi-level caches. For example, if your system says that it has an L1 and an L2 cache, these are a level 1 cache (small and very fast) and a level 2 cache (larger and slower than the L1 cache, but still much smaller and faster than the main memory).

The trouble with RAM and cache memories is that (a) they are expensive compared to other slower forms of storage, (b) they are volatile, which means that their contents go away when you turn off the power, and (c) they are limited in size, and

---

[8] There has been an attempt by standards committees to call 2^{20} bytes a mebibyte (MiB) and reserve the name megabyte for exactly one million bytes. Similarly they suggest a gibibyte (GiB), etc. However so far this hasn't been picked up by the community, and few people would know what you were talking about if you referred to, say, a tebibyte or a TiB. Don Knuth has proposed names like *large terabyte* (TTB) for 2^{30}, but this has also not been generally accepted.

so they can't be used for archival storage of everything that programmers need to save. So you need a more permanent storage solution where you can save big files for as long as you want. There are a number of options for this. All computers now have hard disks, which can be huge. For example, the last disk that I bought, a high speed 1TB backup disk for my Mac, which I bought in May 2008, cost less that $400. Other types of external storage include USB thumb drives, CDs, DVDs, and floppies, although floppies are rapidly disappearing, mainly because of the convenience and price of USB devices. The super-thin Mac Air doesn't even have a CD or DVD because they assume that from now on downloads will all be from the Web, so maybe they are going away as well.

The final component of a computer is its network, which has become a crucial component of modern computing, with network speeds up to a gigabit/second now common and faster networking available. By comparison, the first cross-US network between Stanford and BBN in 1968 ran at about 300 bits/second and cost $50,000 per year for the dedicated phone line.

1.3 What Happens When You Submit a Java Program?

Computers only understand very low-level instructions written in a code called machine language, which is different for every kind of computer, and so unfortunately it doesn't understand instructions that are written in Java, or any other programming language. So somehow the program that you write has to be translated into the very obscure machine language numerical codes that the computer understands. This translation is done by another computer program that for most languages takes your program and translates into machine language, or to a somewhat more readable version called assembly language, which is then converted into machine language by another program called an assembler. Java is somewhat more complicated because it usually compiles into an intermediate language called bytecode, which is then translated into machine language by a bytecode interpreter, but I won't worry about this distinction. So the process to consider is that, when you execute your program on the computer, it will first be translated by another program called the compiler or interpreter into either machine code, assembly code, or bytecode, and assembly code or bytecode will then be translated by another program into machine code.

This process gives rise to two types of errors when you run your program, compile errors and execution errors. Compile errors are those detected by the compiler when it tries to translate your Java program into bytecode; they occur when you submit a Java program that doesn't follow the Java language. For example, if you were to write

```
iff x < 7 small = x
```

instead of the correct Java

```
if (x < 7) small = x;
```

then the compiler can be expected to detect the misspelling of i f and the missing parentheses and semicolon, and give you compile error messages telling you about them. If your program has compile errors, then the computer won't try to run it until you make changes to fix the errors. If your program has no compile errors,, then the computer will run it, at which point it is possible to get run time errors. For example, if you divide x by y and y's value is zero, then the program will stop running with a divide by zero error message, which is called a divide by zero runtime exception.

1.4 Computer Science

Effective programming is part of the discipline called Computer Science, but is only a small part of that field, which as I'll discuss below contains many sub-specialties. It is a field with very high job satisfaction (e.g. in 2007 *Money Magazine* did an analysis of all careers in terms of job satisfaction called *Best Jobs in America*, and put Software Engineer on top of the list[9]). Computer Science is a field that is more diverse than any other field because we have inveigled ourselves into every discipline, and it is a field that has a huge number of available jobs. The large number of available jobs, combined with a reduced number of graduates in Computer Science, has led to very high salaries for new graduates combined, in many cases, with signing bonuses.

Computer Science has many subfields like Artificial Intelligence, Graphics (and its related fields like Visualization, Animation, and Game Development), Databases (and related fields like Data Mining), Simulation, Software Engineering, Networking, Operating Systems, Programming Language Design, Computer Architecture (which overlaps with Computer Engineering), Software and network Security, Robotics, Computer Science Theory, etc. All of them require a strong background in computer programming.

Computer Science has considerable underlying theory that all practitioners must understand to at least some level. For example we can prove that it is mathematically impossible to write programs for some problems. Other problems in a class called NP-Complete problems are believed to have no efficient solutions and so for a reasonably large number of inputs you can't expect to be able to find an accurate solution, and must write a program that looks for a good approximation of

---

[9] University Professor was second.

8

the best solution using *heuristics*. Even for relatively simple programs, how you store your data can have significant effects on the efficiency of the algorithms that process the data, and so Computer Scientists will know different methods for doing this and how to analyze which is the best approach to take for any specific problem.

So if you want to make a career that includes computer programming, I strongly recommend that you consider a degree in Computer Science to provide you with all of the skills that you will need.

1.5 Exercises

At the end of most chapters there will be three types of exercises, general questions about concepts from the chapter, in-lab programming assignments suitable for a two-hour laboratory with teaching assistant help, and out-lab programming assignments suitable for weekly independent programming assignments. This chapter will be an exception; since I haven't yet introduced programming in this chapter, there will just be general questions.

General questions

1. Approximately how many kilobytes are there in a gigabyte?

2. Exactly how many kilobytes are there in a gigabyte?

3. Approximately how many bytes are there in a megabyte?

4. Approximately how many bits are there in a megabyte?

5. As discussed in a footnote, standards committees have attempted to introduce new names that include mebibyte for storage sizes. Exacty how many bytes are in a mebibyte. Give your answer in both decimal and binary.

6. Java uses two bytes to store characters. How many different characters can be stored with this representation?

7. Most previous languages used one byte to store characters. How many different characters can be stored with this representation?

8. Which is faster, a computer's RAM or its cache memory?

9. Which is larger, a computer's RAM or its cache memory?

10. Which is larger, a computer's external storage (e.g., total disk storage) or its RAM?

11. Approximately how far does light travel in one billionth of a second?

12. Why is the speed of light relevant to computer designers?

13. What are two steps that you should always take before beginning to type in your solution to a programming assignment?

14. What are the two general types of errors that a program can have?

15. Give two reasons why we don't use machine language for our programming.

16. What is the role of a Java compiler?

17. If a number is stored using four bytes, how many possible different values could be stored in this number? Give your solution as a power of two.

18. If a number is stored using two bytes, how many possible different values could be stored in this number? Give your solution both as a power of two and as a decimal number.

19. Explain the difference between an algorithm and a program.

20. The text says that it is possible to prove that some problems cannot ever be programmed. Try googling the Turing Halting Problem to see the original example, which predated the first general purpose electronic computers.

Chapter 2. A First Java Program

2.1 Introduction

In this chapter I'll be developing a small Java program, and then in Chapter 3 I'll show how to implement it through BlueJ. The goal isn't that you'll understand all of the details, I'll be getting into them over the next few chapters, but that you'll get a basic understanding of the design process and can then build on for the rest of the book. As I described in the preface of this book, the best way to learn to program is to first see examples of code that you can work through and then get into the underlying details once you have seen how they can be applied.

Java is an object-oriented programming language (OOL). When programming in an OOL like Java, you need to decide what objects you want your program to deal with. For example, if your program is analyzing the statistics for a baseball team then one type of object would be a team. This would probably consist of a list of players on the team, and a player would be another kind of object. The team would also have an owner, coaches, trainers, etc., and if your program needs to deal with them, then they would be different kinds of objects.

Identifying objects will quickly become automatic as you write your first programs. You'll start off by thinking of the objects that you want your program to work on, and will define them in a structure called a *class*. Then you'll usually decide that these objects have sub-pieces (e.g., a baseball team will consist of players, coaches, and other personnel) and so you'll also build classes for them. Classes will be given names that make it clear what they do, and convention says that they will begin with an uppercase letter. So in this case you are likely to have, at first, two classes called `Team` and `Player`.

Once one has decided on the objects that will be in your program, a more advanced step is to decide that some of your objects share some properties. For example, the team needs to pay both players and coaches and to arrange their travel. This leads to a concept called inheritance where you could create a class called, say, `Employee`, that defines these shared properties, and then create subclasses for the `Player` and `Coach` classes that have the components that are unique to them, but also lets them use the components from the Employee parent class. I'll describe inheritance near the end of the book in Chapter 16.

2.2 The Structure of a Class Definition

Think first of the `Player` class. Each team will consist of many players, each of whom will be an instantiation of the `Player` class. We call these instantiations *instances* of the `Player` class or *objects* from the `Player` class. So we need a way to create new player instances. Say, at this point, that all that we want to know about a player is their name, their number of hits, and their number of at bats. For example, we might want to have a statement that does something like

```
new Player("John Adams", 40, 300)
```

which says that John Adams is a new player who currently has 40 hits in 300 at bats. We'll call this use of `Player` a constructor, since it constructs new objects in the `Player` class. In Java we'll want a way to refer to this new `Player` object, and so we'll use statements that have the form:

```
Player jack = new Player("John Adams", 30, 300);
Player greatOne = new Player("Mick Jagger", 245, 355);
```

So when we define the class called `Player`, we'll need to specify what the constructor will do, that is what we want to do when a new player is created. A class will often have more than one constructor, but we won't need that for a while.

I've said that for this first program all that we need to know about a player is their name, number of hits, and number of at bats. We will call these values, which save the critical information about each player, the `Player` class *instance variables* or *instance fields*.

Now that we have information on players, we'd like to do something useful with it. E.g., say that we want to be able to compute a player's batting average. So with the declarations given above, we might want to say "for the player instance named `jack`, compute his batting average" and "for the player named `greatOne`, compute his batting average." In Java this will become `jack.batAvg()` and `greatOne.batAvg()`, where `batAvg()` is called a *method* that is being applied to the `jack` and `greatOne` objects. So we'll need to define this method in the `Player` class to say how a batting average is computed given what we know about the player, which is their name, number of hits, and number of at bats (we'll divide the number of hits by the number of at bats).

All of this gives an expectation of what we expect a new class definition to look like. It will have four major parts, the header, which describes and names the class; the instance fields, which store any critical information about the objects; constructors,

12

which tell what happens when we make a new instance of the class; and methods, which use the instance fields to compute new values.

As a result, Java's class definition will usually have the form:

```
public class ClassName
{
    instance field definitions
    constructor definitions
    method definitions
}
```

I'll look at each of these components in the following four sections:

2.3 The Class Header

By convention class names will usually begin with an uppercase letter, as discussed earlier, and if the name consists of multiple words, like `ClassName`, then subsequent words in the name will also begin with an uppercase letter. Other letters in the name, as shown, will be lowercase. { and } braces are being used to begin and end the body of the class definition. In Java groups of instructions, called *blocks*, are grouped between braces like this. The only unexpected word here is probably the word `public`. This is called an *access specifier* and says that other pieces of the program can use this class. In the unusual situation where a class cannot be directly accessed by other parts of the program, this access specifier would be `private` instead of `public`.[10]

2.4 The Instance Fields

Instance fields contain the information that describes the object that is being created. For the `Player` class this will be, at this time, the player's name, number of hits, and number of at bats. In Java we'll declare these with the statements:

```
String name;
int hits,
    atBats;
```

The first line says that the player's name will be called `name` and that its type will be `String`. A string is denoted with the form "my string" where the double quotes are called the string delimiters. The delimiters aren't part of the string, and so, for example, the string "Denbigh Starkey" has 15 characters, the 14 letters and the

---

[10] There are two other access specifiers, default and protected, but don't be concerned with those yet.

space, and "cat" has three characters. We saw strings earlier when they were used to give the names in the constructor examples (e.g., "John Adams").

The next two lines declare that both hits and atBats are variables that have type int. This means that they can take on integer values. I could have also declared them with two declarations using:

```
int hits;
int atBats;
```

Note that when I declared them with one statement, the two variables were separated with a comma, but when I used two declarations, they were both terminated with semicolons.

This is a good time to mention that Java is free format. This means that Java statements can be typed in without regard to line boundaries, and so the instance fields could have been typed in as:

```
      String
                 name;int
hits, atBats;
```

without any difference in meaning, but obviously it is a lot less readable. What you should do is to make your programs as readable as possible, and I'll be showing how to type in your program to make it easier to read.

Two additional good practices are to always use names for your variables that make it clear what they do and to also add comments whenever a variable is declared that explains what it does in more detail. There are two ways of adding a comment in Java. The one that we'll use first is that anything after // on a line will be treated as a comment to the reader and ignored by Java. For example,

```
String name;   // the player's full name
int hits,      // the player's current number of hits
    atBats;    // the player's current number of at bats
```

has the same meaning as the declarations without the comments, and makes it much easier for another person reading the program to see what is going on.

Remember that by convention class names begin with uppercase letters, but, as is shown here, by convention variable names begin with a lowercase letter. If they consist of multiple words, then either each word after the first will begin with an uppercase letter (e.g., atBats, as I've been using) or an underscore will be used to separate the words (e.g., at_bats). I'll be using the uppercase approach, but either is acceptable. Method names, by convention, follow the same rules as variables, and will begin with a lowercase letter.

14

2.5 Constructor Definition

When we use statements like:

```
Player jack = new Player("John Adams", 30, 300);
Player greatOne = new Player("Mick Jagger", 245, 355);
```

we are using the `Player` class constructor to create two new objects (or instances) of the class. Note that the constructor name will always be the same as the class name, because the constructor is being used to create new objects in the class. The code for the constructor in the `Player` class will be:

```
public Player(String in_name, int in_hits, int in_atBats)
    {
        // initialize instance fields
        name = in_name;
        hits = in_hits;
        atBats = in_atBats;
    }
```

To understand this, you must understand the three statements that have the form:

```
lhs = rhs;
```

This is called an assignment statement, and its meaning is to compute the value of the right-hand side (rhs) and make that the new value of the variable, which is on the left-hand side (lhs). So if, say, in_hits has the value 125 then the assignment statement shown above makes that the new value of hits.

Consider the two declarations where we created two new `Player` objects named jack and greatOne. When we say, for example,

```
Player jack = new Player("John Adams", 30, 300);
```

we are saying that we want this object's name field to be "John Adams", its hits field to be 30, and its atBats field to be 300. "John Adams", 30, and 300 are called the actual parameters, which matched up with the formal parameters in_name, in_hits, and in_atBats in the header of the constructor definition. The three assignment statements in the constructor then give the instance fields name, hits, and atBats the correct values.

Later, when we create the greatOne player with

```
Player greatOne = new Player("Mick Jagger", 245, 355);
```

the formal parameters for this object will be given the values "Mick Jagger", 245, and 355, and they will then be assigned as the values of greatOne's name, atBats, and hits instance fields.

As this example has shown, if a formal parameter corresponds to an instance field in a constructor, then my preference is to give it the same name as the instance field except that I add in_ to its beginning. This is a personal preference and not a Java convention. Another common alternative is to give it exactly the same name, but the problem with this is that it leads to incorrect assignment statements like:

```
name = name;
hits = hits;
atBats = atBats;
```

To get around the problems that this would cause, Java provides a keyword this, which says that if you precede a variable name with the qualifier this, then you are referring to the instance field in the class. So you would write these as

```
this.name = name;
this.hits = hits;
this.atBats  = atBats;
```

However, I think that you'll find that preceding the parameter names with in_ will be less confusing.

2.6 Method Declarations

The final part of our class definition is the place where we define methods. A method takes the information in the object's instance fields and returns information about them to the rest of the program. This information could be very simple like returning the value of one of the instance fields, or more complex like computing the player's batting average by dividing the player's hits instance field value by their atBats instance field value. In this case I'll just have a single method called batAvg(), as discussed earlier, which computes the player's batting average. The code for this will be:

```
public double batAvg()
{
    double average;
    average = (double) hits / atBats;
    return average;
}
```

This contains a number of new features and some familiar ones. I'll start with the familiar ones.

The access control is public because we want other parts of the program to be able to use this method. I am using { and } to surround the code for the method, just as we did with both the class definition and the constructor definition.

The three main new features are the word double, which is used in two ways, the return keyword, and the / symbol in the hits / atBats expression.

The keyword double in the header says that when we say, for example, jack.batAvg() or greatOne.batAvg(), as discussed earlier, then the values that we want are floating point numbers like, in this case 0.100 for jack since he had 30 hits in 300 at bats, and 0.690 for greatOne since he has 245 hits in 355 at bats. So if we have a number, it will usually have one of two types, either int, in which case it will be an integer without a decimal point, or it will be a double, in which case it will be a floating point number (i.e., it will have a decimal point). Since the result of computing a batting average will be a floating point number, we declare this by saying that batAvg() is a double, as shown in the method header.

We want the method to return the value of the batting average as its value (e.g., 0.690 for greatOne), so we do this with the statement:

```
return expression_that_computes_the_batting_average;
```

where the expression has a double (floating point) value.

To compute the batting average, we want to divide hits by atBats. The divide operator on Java, and in nearly all other programming languages, isn't the traditional ÷ operator, because that doesn't exist on most keyboards, but is / instead. So hits / atBats computes this for us. Unfortunately in Java this will return an integer value and throw away any fractional part, so we have to first convert the value of hits into a double with (double) hits. This type conversion is called a cast, but don't worry about that too much now. I'll get back into this later in much more detail in the chapter on assignment statements and arithmetic expressions. I've assigned the value of this expression to a variable called average, which I've first declared to have type double, and than have returned that value as the value returned by the method.

I could have been more concise and directly returned the ratio of hits to at bats with the definition:

```
public double batAvg()
{
    return (double) hits / atBats;
}
```

but I've used the longer version for clarity.

2.7 The Complete Class Definition

Now I've covered all of the pieces, the complete class definition is:

```
public class Player
{
    // instance fields
    private String name;   // player's name
    private int hits,      // player's number of hits
               atBats;     // player's number of at bats

    // Constructor for objects of class Player1
    public Player(String in_name, int in_hits, int in_atBats)
    {
        // initialize instance fields
        name = in_name;
        hits = in_hits;
        atBats = in_atBats;
    }

    // method to compute the player's batting average
    public double batAvg()
    {
        double average;  // batting average
        average = (double) hits / atBats;
        return average;
    }
}
```

2.8 Encapsulation

Encapsulation is the programming concept that in many ways underlies Object-Oriented Programming. It says that objects are instances of classes, and that users of the objects should only have access to certain information about them. That is, constructors, methods, instance fields, and class fields will be declared to be public or private, and users will have no access to private components. This lets a programmer completely change the implementation of one of their classes without affecting the user code, which will not have access to internal implementation details of the class.

This is similar to the concept called *abstraction*. For example, say we have a list of objects. It is easier for the user to understand this, and the operations like adding a value to the list or checking to see whether a particular value is in the list, if these can be described without having to know how they work. Few of us, for example, would be able to drive a car if we had to know everything that was happening when we moved the wheel or pushed on the brake.

Encapsulation is often summarized as the property that users should only have access to the information that they need.

18

As part of the encapsulation philosophy, instance fields should be defined as being private. For example, this means that a user of the Player class cannot directly access an object's name, hits, or atBats instance fields. If you want a user to access these values, that access should be through a method that you provide. For example, you will often have a method in the Player class called getName() with the definition:

```
public String getName()
{
    return name;
}
```

and then jack.getName() would have the value "John Adams".

2.9 A Summary of the Design Process Used in the Player Class Definition

A lot has gone on here. I'll now summarize the major features.

1. When you begin your program design, the first thing that you do is to decide on the objects that you want your program to manipulate. It is worth spending time on this to get it right, since if you change your mind later, you might waste much of the time that you spent before making the change. Once you have decided on your objects, you design a class for each of them.
2. Each class that you create can be instantiated to create objects of the class. These objects are called instances of the class. For each class in your program you'll take the actions described in the rest of these numbered paragraphs.
3. The next step, for each class, is to decide on the information that you want to save about the objects of that class. This should include all of the information about your objects that the program will need, and nothing more. For example, if I'd needed to compute the on base percentage for a player, this information would have to include the number of walks that the player had. These pieces of information become your instance fields, and their declarations will usually be the first thing in your class definition. Their access specifier should be private, which will mean that they cannot be accessed directly but only through methods that you supply.
4. The next thing to do is to write the constructor. As we'll see later, a class might have more than one constructor, but for a while I'll only use one. The major goal of the constructor is to provide values for the instance fields. This is called initializing the instance fields. In most cases this will be done through actual parameters when an object is instantiated. Stick to a consistent way of naming your constructor formal parameters. For example, if I have an instance field called fred, then I will name the corresponding constructor formal parameter in_fred, which will have the same type as

fred (e.g., String, int, or double). Then in the constructor code I'll have a statement fred = in_fred; Many programmers replace this with the line this.fred = fred; but some programmers can get confused by this.

5. This just leaves the methods. There should be a method for any information that you need about the instance fields in the object. If a method returns a value (e.g., batAvg() in my example program), then the type of that return value (e.g., int, double, or String) will be declared in the method header, and there will be a return statement in the method, which returns a value of that type. We haven't seen it yet, but if a method does something without returning a value, then the type will be declared as void and there won't be a return statement.

That covers the basics of writing a class. Now I'll be spending several chapters getting into a lot of the underlying details. First, however, I'll show you how to get this class into BlueJ and use it both directly and also through another class, which will be called a unit test class.

2.10 Exercises

General questions

1. By convention, which of the following would be good names for Java classes? MyClass, my_Class, myClass, myclass, MYCLASS?

2. If I am declaring a class called Fred, what will its header usually be?

3. In the class Fred, what are the three major components in Fred's definition block?

4. What does the constructor do?

5. What symbols are used around the components of a class definition to show the beginning and end of the body of the definition?

6. What do methods do?

7. What is the purpose of the instance fields?

8. Will instance fields usually be public or private? Why?

9. If I have a statement like x = 7; // x is 7, what does the // do?

10. Do instance field names usually begin with an upper-case letter, a lower-case letter, or a digit?

11. Do class names usually begin with an upper-case letter, a lower-case letter, or a digit?

12. Do method names usually begin with an upper-case letter, a lower-case letter, or a digit?

13. Do variable names usually begin with an upper-case letter, a lower-case letter, or a digit?

14. What is encapsulation?

15. If I want users of my class to be able to access an instance field and it is private, how can I let them get its value?

16. If three objects are instances of the same class, will their instance fields usually have the same values or different values?

17. How many instances of a class can be made?

18. If `fredsMethod()` is a method defined in the class `Student` and `john` is an instance (object) of this class, how do I apply the method to `john`?

19. If you have defined a class called `Cricketer` with two instance fields, `name` and `testAverage`, how would you create three new objects in that class called tendulkar, cowdrey, and bradman? The names of the three players are `Colin Cowdrey`, `Sachin Tendulkar`, and `Donald Bradman`, and their test match averages were `44.06`, `54.98`, and `99.94`, respectively.

20. Given the `Player` class developed in this chapter, what is the name of the principle that says that its instance fields should only be accessed through methods that return their values?

In-lab programs

1. The `Player` class in Section 2.7 had one method, `batAvg()`. In my description of encapsulation I mentioned that, since instance fields are private, it is usual for classes to have methods that give access to the values of the instance fields, and gave an example of a method `getName()` to do this. Write methods

that return the values of the `hits` and `atBats` fields.

2. A class named `MyClass` has one instance field named `myField` that has type `int`, and has a single method called `getMyField()` that returns the value of `myField` as an `int`. The value of `myField` is provided by the constructor. Write the full definition of the class.

Out-lab programs

1. Write a class named `Student` that has three instance fields, `name` (`String`), `creditsComplete` (`int`), and `gradePoints` (`int`). Write four methods for the class, `public double gpa()` which returns the value of `gradePoints` divided by `creditsComplete`, and `getname()`, `getCreditsComplete()`, and `getGradePoints()`, which return the values of the three fields.

2. Add a method `creditsRemain()` to the `Student` class in out-lab 1, above, that returns an `int` that gives the student's remaining credits, which can be found by subtracting `creditsComplete` from 120. The subtraction operator in Java is the traditional -, so to, say, subtract b from a, you use a – b.

Chapter 3. Implementing and Testing the Player Class under BlueJ

3.1 Bringing up BlueJ

Before you can use the code, you'll need to bring up BlueJ on your computer. If it isn't already installed, along with a recent Java Development Kit (JDK), follow the instructions in Appendix A to download the packages. Once this is done, bring up BlueJ and under the Project pulldown, select New Project. BlueJ will ask for a project name (choose something that you will recognize) and a directory where you will save this project. I recommend creating a special directory for all of your Java programs, with subdirectories for major subprojects. The window will look like:

This, and subsequent screenshots, are from a Mac, but the window is very similar if you are using BlueJ in a Windows or Linux environment.

Existing projects in this directory (which is named Example in this case) will be shown in the main window, but since this is the first project in the Example directory it will be blank, as shown. I've selected Player as the name of the new project.

When I click Create, I'll get the main BlueJ project window, which in this case will be:

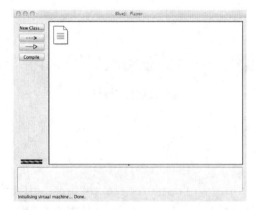

The icon with four horizontal lines is for a project READ_ME file, which I'll ignore for a while. Click on the New Class button and you'll get a window:

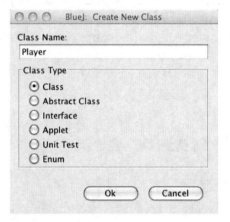

where I have named this class Player. Hit Ok and BlueJ will add an icon for this class to the main project window, which will now be:

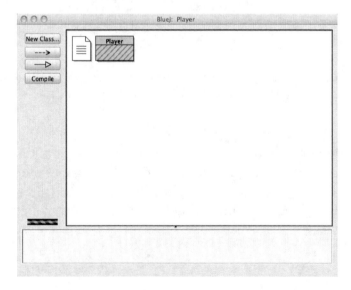

Now we can type in the code for the `Player` class. Double click on the `Player` class icon and you will get the following code template:

```
/**
 * Write a description of class Player here.
 *
 * @author (your name)
 * @version (a version number or a date)
 */
public class Player
{
    // instance variables - replace the example below with your own
    private int x;

    /**
     * Constructor for objects of class Player
     */
    public Player()
    {
        // initialise instance variables
        x = 0;
    }

    /**
     * An example of a method - replace this comment with your own
     *
     * @param  y    a sample parameter for a method
     * @return      the sum of x and y
     */
    public int sampleMethod(int y)
    {
        // put your code here
        return x + y;
    }
}
```

Don't worry about the material between /** and */ groupings for now; anything that is between /* and */ is a comment, and the /** form is a special comment that is tied into Java's automatic documentation system. Note that the code template has made some assumptions. It assumes that this is a `public` class with the name that you gave when you set up the class icon (`Player`), that you will have private instance fields, that there will be a constructor with the same name as the class, that its primary role is to initialize[11] the instance fields, and that there will be at least one public method.

_____

[11] BlueJ is developed in England and Australia so it uses the English spelling "initialise."

25

So edit this file by selecting text with your mouse and replacing it, and follow the instructions in the /** to */ blocks, to get the code so that it is something like the following, where I have used my name and the current date, which you should replace.

```java
/**
 * Player class
 * First demo program
 *
 * @author Denbigh Starkey
 * @version 5/7/09
 */
public class Player
{
    // instance fields
    private String name;   // Player's name
    private int hits,      // Player's number of hits
                atBats;    // Player's number of at bats

    /**
     * Constructor for objects of class Player
     */
    public Player(String in_name, int in_hits, int in_atBats)
    {
        // initialise instance fields
        name = in_name;
        hits = in_hits;
        atBats = in_atBats;
    }

    /**
     * Compute the player's batting average
     *
     * @return      hits divided by at bats.
     */
    public double batAvg()
    {
        return (double) hits / atBats;
    }
}
```

Now go back to the main project window and click the `Compile` button. If you've typed in everything correctly,, you'll get a message at the bottom saying "class compiled - no syntax errors" which means that the compile was successful. If, however, you made a mistake when typing in the program, when you hit the `Compile` button, you'll get an error message and the problem area will be highlighted. For example, say you typed the line

```java
atBats = in_atBats;
```

as

```java
atBats = in_atbats;
```

you will get:

```
                                        Player
 Compile   Undo   Cut   Copy   Paste   Find...   Find Next   Close        Source Code   ▼

    * Player class
    * First demo program
    *
    * @author Denbigh Starkey
    * @version 5/7/08
    */
   public class Player
   {
       // instance variables
       private String name;
       private int hits,
                   at_bats;

       /**
        * Constructor for objects of class Player
        */
       public Player(String in_name, int in_hits, int in_at_bats)
       {
           // initialise instance variables
           name = in_name;
           hits = in_hits;
           at_bats = in_atbats;
       }

       /**
        * Compute the player's batting average
        *
        * @return     hits divided by at bats as a double
        */
       public double bat_avg()
       {
           return (double) hits / at_bats;
       }
   }

 cannot find symbol - variable in_atbats                              ?    saved
```

The message at the bottom, cannot find symbol - variable in_atbats, is showing the problem and the line where the problem occurred has been highlighted. When this happens (which it usually will), correct the problem and then hit the Compile button again until the compile is successful.

Now we can test our class. First we need some objects in the class. Right-click on the class icon and you'll get a popup window:

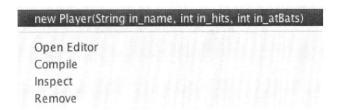

new Player(String in_name, int in_hits, int in_atBats)

Open Editor
Compile
Inspect
Remove

Click in the new Player line and BlueJ will let you construct an object in a new window:

27

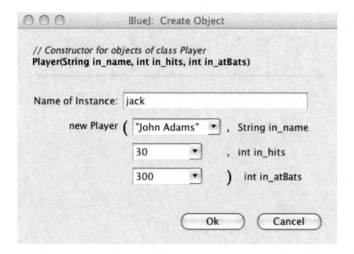

Enter the object information as shown, and do this twice, once for John Adams and once for Mick Jagger. The main project window will now contain:

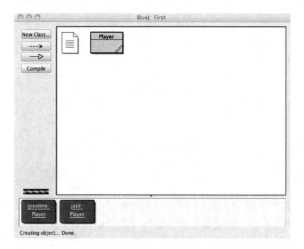

where icons for the two objects now show at the bottom.

Now say that we want to know what John Adams' batting average is. Right-click on jack's icon and you'll get another popup:

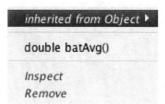

and if you select the batAvg() method, it will give you his batting average, which is 0.1, with the output window:

28

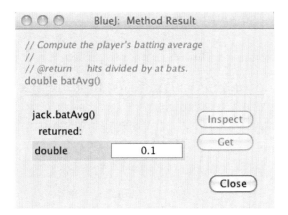

So in summary we have, over the last two chapters, designed a Java class and implemented it using BlueJ. We have then tested the class by instancing objects in the class and testing the only class method, batAvg(), on those objects.

This is a somewhat simplified approach when compared to what will happen in more complicated programs. Most programs will consist of a number of classes that interrelate (e.g., we could have a Team class that contained a list of players from the Player class). There will also usually be a class whose purpose is to test out all of the classes. This will often be called a unit test class. The testing process will then usually be done at two levels; we can, as we implement additional classes, individually test them using the approach that I took with the Player class, or we can have a unit test class that tests all of our classes, which I'll introduce in Sections 3.3 and 3.4.

3.2 Output Statements, System.out.print() and System.out.println()

In the unit test class I'll need to be able to output the values of expressions and variables. Java has several ways in which a programmer can do input and output, which is always just called I/O. In this section I'll be looking at two methods that are part of Java, System.out.print() and System.out.println(). In Chapter 10 I'll describe much more powerful ways to control your I/O, including the use of formatted output and I/O through dialog boxes and in Chapter 18 I'll describe ways to retrieve data from, and send data to, external files, which will typically be on disk, which is called file I/O.

System.out.print() and System.out.println() provide unformatted output of values and strings. This means, for example, that if you try

```
double x = 3.0 / 7;
System.out.println(x);  // as we'll see this prints the value of x
```

29

then you'll get as output something similar to:

```
0.42857142857142855
```

This is probably a lot more numerical precision than you wanted, and so in Chapter 10 I'll show how to control the output, using `System.out.format()`. For example, you might use it to tell Java that you want the number output rounded to three decimal places, so in this case the output would be:

```
0.429
```

Until then I'll use unformatted output. If you want more control, then skip ahead to Chapter 10 and read how to get better control of your output.

3.2.1 Method call notation

Before getting into the details of the two unformatted output methods I need to cover the meaning of more complex Java method calls. The two methods that I'll be using here are `System.out.print()` and `System.out.println()`. The first thing to notice is that there is a notational addition. When I had the `batAvg()` method earlier, and wanted to apply it to the object `jack` I used `jack.batAvg()`. Here the methods are `println()` and `print()`, but they are preceded by an object that has two components instead of one, `System` and `out`. This structure is important to undestand. When the part preceding the method has two components like this, then it is telling Java where to find the object called `out`, which in this case is in a class called `System`. A predefined class like this is a collection of related objects and methods that have been predefined for you in Java. This class, `System`, is always available to your programs. So in summary, if you have a method call like `b.c()`, then `c()` is a method that is operating on an object named `b` in your program; if you have a call like `A.b.c()`, then `c()` is a method that is being applied to an object named `b` that is defined in the class named `A`.

In this case the Java class called `System` includes (along with a lot of other useful stuff) an object named `out` and two methods named `print()` and `println()` that can operate on `out`.

A final notational addition is that a method can have zero or more actual parameters that are placed between its parentheses. In our example `batAvg()` had no actual parameters and so it was called as, for example, `jack.batAvg()`. The `print()` and `println()` methods both have a single actual parameter, which is the thing that you want to print out. If we want to output, say, the value of the variable x using `print()`, then the code will be `System.out.print(x);`. So a method call will be

30

working on an object, which is called the implicit parameter, but will also usually have additional actual parameters placed between its parentheses that provide additional information. Even if a method has actual parameters it is common, when discussing it, to refer to it with empty parentheses, as I have for `print()` and `println()`, above.

3.2.2 System.out.println()

Now that the structural details of the method calls are out of the way, we can look at the details of the two unformatted output methods starting with `System.out.println()`. The method has a single actual parameter that contains the value that you want to be output, and the value will be output and the current output line will be ended. So, for example, if you use:

```
int x = -345;
System.out.ptintln("The value of x is:");
System.out.println(x);
Sysem.out.println("The value of 3x is:");
System.out.println(3 * x);
```

Then BlueJ creates a popup output window (if it doesn't already exist from a previous output) and prints:

```
The value of x is:
-345
The value of 3x is:
-1035
```

in that window. In the first and third calls the actual parameter is a string that prints out exactly as shown. In the second call it is an integer variable and in the fourth it is an integer valued expression. The actual parameter can be pretty much anything in Java, but will most commonly be a string or one of the various numerical types that we'll see in more deail in Chapter 5, or string or numerical expressions.

You'll often find that the output window needs to be cleaned out before a new run. If you click in the output window, then BjueJ gives you an option to clear this window.

3.2.3 System.out.print()

`System.out.print()` is similar to `System.out.println()`, with the difference being that it doesn't end the current line. Subsequent outputs will be added to the line until a `System.out.println()` ends it at which point the output will appear on the output window. It is, therefore, usually used intermingled with `System.out.println()` calls. For example, if one has:

```
int x = -345;
System.out.ptint("The value of x is: ");
System.out.println(x);
System.out.print("The value of 3x is: ");
System.out.println(3 * x);
```

then the output will be:

```
The value of x is: -345
The value of 3x is: -1035
```

Note that I added a space after the colon in each string output statement that appeared in the output before the -.

println() calls are said to clear the output buffer. print() calls put values into this buffer, and the output line will not be complete until a println() call.

Another option is to use Java's + operator on strings, which I'll describe in more detail in Chapter 6. For now the main thing that you need to know about it is that in print() or println() calls it joins two output values together. This is called concatenation. For example, the last example could be written as:

```
int x = -345;
System.out.ptintln("The value of x is: " + x);
System.out.println("The value of 3x is: " + (3 * x));
```

The parentheses around 3 * x are optional, but they improve readability.

3.3 Testing the Player Class with a UnitTest Class

I'll use the BlueJ techniques used earlier to create a new class called UnitTest with the code shown on the next page.

There are a number of new things here. The class UnitTest has no instance fields or constructors, but just has a single method called main(), which is public, static, and void. We want to be able to use it, so it is public, not private. As discussed earlier, any method that does something but doesn't return a value will be declared as void. The static declaration is a bit technical; if a method isn't operating on an object, and since it doesn't have a constructor, the UnitTest class can't have an object, has to be declared as static. For now just use this header in your main() method and don't worry about it.

32

```
/**
 * Unit test of the Player class.
 *
 * @author Denbigh Starkey
 * @version 5/7/09
 */
public class UnitTest
{
    public static void main()
    {
        String jackName = "John Adams",
                greatOneName = "Mick Jagger";
        Player jack = new Player(jackName, 30, 300);
        Player greatOne = new Player(greatOneName, 25, 40);
        System.out.print(jackName);
        System.out.print("'s batting average is ");
        System.out.println(jack.batAvg());
        System.out.print(greatOneName);
        System.out.print("'s batting average is ");
        System.out.println(greatOne.batAvg());
    }
}
```

Any complete Java program will have a class containing a `main()` method. When Java executes the program, it will do so at the `main()` method. This is hidden somewhat when using an integrated development environment like BlueJ.

You will usually see the header of the `main()` method as:

```
public static void main(String[] args)
```

This lets you add extra information called command line arguments when you run your Java program. This is an advanced feature and so I'll use the simpler form without the `String[] args` parameter, as shown above.

To run the program, which now has both the `UnitTest` and the `Player` class, right-click on the `UnitTest` class and select main to run. The output will then appear in a pop-up window.

3.4 Unit Testing With JUnit

In the last section I introduced the concept of having a unit test `main()` method to test your class. Although this is a common approach for small programs, it doesn't scale up well as the number of classes in your program increases. In this section I'll introduce an approach that is often better, which is to use the Java utility called JUnit. I recommend that you get into the habit of using JUnit even at this early stage, as it will make your life much easier down the line.

Say that you have a medium-sized Java program that contains 50 classes. If you use the approach of having a unit test main() method, then you will have to put in exhaustive test cases for all of these classes in the main method and any time that you change any one of the 50 classes, you'll have to run the main() method that runs test cases on all of the methods, which could take a while.

Another approach is pure unit testing where you come up with a comprehensive set of test cases for each class as it is developed, and then any time that you modify a class you have a mechanism that lets you just run the test cases for that class. This is the approach that is called unit testing. Java has a very useful application called JUnit, which is fully supported under BlueJ, that lets you do this.

I'll give an example that demonstrates the basics of JUnit. Say that we want to implement a class to convert between different kinds of temperatures. To keep things simple I'll just convert a Fahrenheit value to the closest integral centigrade value. A class to do this could be:

```java
/**
 * Contains a single instance field, which is a Fahrenheit temperature.
 * Methods manipulate this temperature
 *
 * @author Denbigh Starkey
 * @version 10/15/08
 */
public class Temperature
{

    //instance field
    private int fahrenheit;

    /**
     * Constructor for objects of class Temperature
     */
    public Temperature(int in_fahrenheit)
    {
        // initialize instance field
        fahrenheit = in_fahrenheit;
    }

    /**
     * Convert the Fahrenheit temperature to centigrade
     *
     * @return the closest centigrade equivalent of the Fahrenheit val.
     */
    public int convertToCent()
    {
        return (int) Math.round((fahrenheit - 32) / 1.8);
    }
}
```

Don't worry about the (int) Math.round(expression) part at this point. It is a method called round() in a built-in class called Math that returns the closest integer value to the value of the expression inside the parentheses.

Now that we have this class, we want to test it. First, in the usual BlueJ window, select the New Class option. This gives the popup window

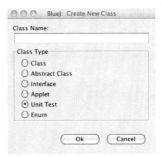

I have selected the Unit Test option. Now select a Class Name. By convention I will give the JUnit test the name of the class that I am testing followed by the word Test, so in this case I'll call it `TemperatureTest`. Then click Ok. BlueJ will give a class with header information, a constructor, and two methods called `setup()` and `teardown()`. For now I'll keep things simple; delete the constructor and the two methods and replace them with the method `testTemperature()` shown below.

```
/**
 * The test class TemperatureTest.
 *
 * @author  Denbigh Starkey
 * @version 8/10/09
 */
public class TemperatureTest extends junit.framework.TestCase
{
    public void testTemperature()
    {
        Temperature freezing = new Temperature(32),
                    boiling = new Temperature(212),
                    equal = new Temperature(-40);
        assertEquals(freezing.convertToCent(), 0);
        assertEquals(boiling.convertToCent(), 100);
        assertEquals(equal.convertToCent(), -40);
    }
}
```

The material outside the method `testTemperature()` will have been provided by BlueJ.

Now we get to the code in the JUnit test class. I've created three `Temperature` objects named `freezing`, `boiling`, and `equal` whose Fahrenheit instance fields are 32, 212, and -40. If the `Temperature` class is working correctly, when I use its `convertToCent()` method on these three objects, I should get 0, 100, and -40 as their centigrade equivalents. When I use the `TestTemperature` class, I have the statements:

```
assertEquals(freezing.convertToCent(), 0);
assertEquals(boiling.convertToCent(), 100);
assertEquals(equal.convertToCent(), -40);
```

which state that these are the values expected.

The class diagram now looks like:

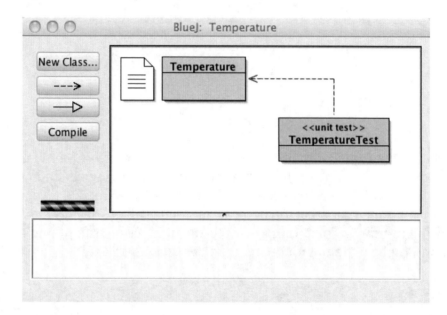

Right-click on the test class and you'll get a drop-down, which lets you select Test Temperature. Do this and, if all of the tests succeed, then you'll get a message telling you that. If, however, one or more tests fail, then you'll get a new popup window with a failure count.

Documentation on JUnit can be found at http://junit.org/junit/javadoc/4.5/. This uses the JavaDocs format, which I'll be describing later in the book. For now go there, click on Assert in the lower left pane, and scan through the methods available, which will show in the main pane.

If you use assertEquals() on two doubles or on a double and an int, you must be careful. For example, say x contains 1.99999999999999 and you use assertEquals(x, 2.0). Probably x is actually 2.0, but due to a roundoff error it is slightly different, and the test will fail. To avoid this problem, every time that you compare the values of two double values, or a double and an int, use another form of the assertEquals() method which has a third parameter called the tolerance. If one or both of x and y are doubles, then to compare them in a JUnit test use something like:

```
assertEquals(x, y, 1.0E-10);
```

36

which will check whether the two values are within 10^{-10} of each other. Sometimes the tolerance that you use will be larger. For example, if you are writing a method to compute baseball batting averages, then you might test it by looking up Ichiru Suzuki's current number of hits and at bats and then seeing whether your result is the same as that posted in the newspaper. Unfortunately if you try

```
assertEquals(batAvg(165, 455), 0.363, 1.0E-10);
```

then the test will fail because the newspaper is already rounding the average to three decimal places. So her you would want to use:

```
assertEquals(batAvg(165, 455), 0.363, 0.001);
```

3.5 Testing Strategies

When you are unit testing your program, the values that you select for your unit test are important. In particular you should test for both normal and abnormal values, and should always test for any boundary values. I'll give a simple example.

Say that you are writing a method that processes prime numbers greater than zero. Your unit test should include normal cases, which in this case are primes like 31 and 117. The test should also make sure that your program behaves well if it is given abnormal values (non-primes) like 30, 100, and -31. Finally you should always include boundary cases, which in this case means values at or very close to 1 since this is the only value boundary. So a minimal test suite for this method would be something like 31, 117, 30, 100, -100, -31, 0, 1, 2. It is important to always select values from these three kinds of inputs, normal, abnormal, and boundary. All of the methods in a class should have unit test suites that cover these three areas.

Even though you attempt to include all reasonable kinds of test data in your unit test, at some point large programs will fail anyway. When you find an input that causes a failure, it should be permanently added to your test suite, even if you are sure that you've fixed the bug. The assumption is that future code modifications could reintroduce the same bug scenario.

Initially your methods will have problems testing for abnormal values, because currently you haven't seen enough Java to be able to code concepts like "if this value is outside the expected range, take this action or return this special value." Later in the book I'll be introducing conditional statements that let you do this.

It is important to recognize that unit testing is only one of many testing strategies that are used in parallel. However all testing strategies include unit testing. For example, interface testing tests the interfaces between units; there are regression testing, smoke testing, black, white, and gray box testing, etc. How to test large programs is one part of the subdiscipline of Computer Science that is called Software Engineering.

3.6 Exercises

General questions

1. In the method call Fred.jane.john(x, y); what is the name of the method?

2. In the method call Fred.jane.john(x, y); what is/are the implicit parameter(s)?

3. In the method call Fred.jane.john(x, y); what is/are the actual parameter(s)?

4. In the method call Fred.jane.john(x, y); what object(s) is/are the method being applied to?

5. In the method call Fred.jane.john(x, y); where is/are the object(s) defined?

6. If you are using JUnit in a Java program that contains eight other classes, not including a possible class that contains main(), how many unit test classes should there be in addition to these classes?

7. In this book my main() methods have the header public static void main(). What is a more common approach?

8. Why is the main() method usually (a) public, (b) static, and (c) void?

9. Explain why using JUnit is often a better approach than using a main class for testing your classes.

10. In a JUnit class, when you are checking to make sure that a double variable named fred has the value 2.5, why is it poor programming to use assertEquals(fred, 2.5);? What would be a better approach?

11. If you are writing a method that is supposed to work for any even value between 100 and 200, what would be a reasonable set of test cases.

12. What will be output by the following code segment?

```
int x,
    y;
x = 2;
y = -15;
System.out.print(x);
System.out.println(y);
System.out.println(3 * x);
```

13. What will be output by the following code segment?

```
int x = 13;
double y = 3.14159;
System.out.print("x: ");
System.out.print(x);
System.out.println(", and y is ");
System.out.println(y);
```

In-lab programs

1. Modify the Temperature class so that instead of converting the instance field from Fahrenheit to centigrade it converts from centigrade to Fahrenheit. Run your program under BlueJ.

2. Implement and test the Player class from in-lab program 1 in Chapter 2.

Out-lab programs

1. The conversion between temperatures in centigrade and Kelvin is that the increments are the same but absolute zero is -273°C and 0°K. For example, 100°C is 373°K. Modify the Temperature class so that the instance field is a temperature as before, but there will now be six methods to convert between the three types. For example, one of the six will be centToKelvin(), which will interpret the instance field as a centigrade value and will return its Kelvin equivalent.

2. Use a main unit test class to test the class that you defined in Out-lab program 1, above.

3. Use JUnit to test the class that you defined in Out-lab program 1, above.

4. Implement the program from out-lab Question 1 in Chapter 2, and test it with

both a `main()` method and a JUnit class.

5. Implement the program from out-lab Question 2 in Chapter 2, and test it with both a `main()` method and a JUnit class.

Chapter 4. Debugging Your Program

4.1 Introduction

As I've discussed earlier, once your program has been designed and typed in through BlueJ, you will confidently expect it to run correctly, but this will almost never happen. First you will get compile errors, which is where the Java compiler being used by BlueJ determines that one or more of the statements in your program isn't legal Java. You will get error messages through BlueJ, which won't let you run your program until all of the compile errors are fixed. Once you've done this, you'll usually get execution errors. There are three major classifications of execution errors, those that cause execution to stop prematurely (e.g., dividing by zero or accessing the sixth element of a structure that only has five elements), those where execution apparently terminates normally but the output is incorrect (e.g., your program is computing the area of a circle with radius 5 and outputs the area of a circle with radius 5 is -103.54), and those where your program goes into an infinite loop and sits there turning its wheels without ever stopping. In this chapter I'll look at where these errors come from and how you will attempt to fix them.

4.2 Compile Errors

When you enter a Java statement that isn't correct, you will get a compile error. When I first started programming, I had at best daily turnaround (and weekly turnaround for production runs) when I submitted a program, and so I carefully checked my programs for typos and similar errors so that I wouldn't waste a day or more. Now most programmers are fairly sloppy with this and rely on the compiler to find any obvious errors. This can lead to problems. If, for example, you have two int variables in your program named x and y and instead of typing x = 7;, you type y = 7;, then you won't get a compile error but later you are likely to have an execution error that might be hard to chase down. Consider the following attempt at a Java program and see how many compile errors that you can find (there are four):

```
/*
 * A program that started with four errors
 * Remember to use */ to end this comment
*/

public class HelloWorld
{
    public static void main();
    {
        System.out.printline("Hello World!")
    }
}
```

41

Some Java systems will attempt to find all of the compile errors at once, which can become confusing, but BlueJ will try to find just one, highlight the place where it occurred, and give you a message. Once you fix it Java will then attempt to find a second, and so on until all compile errors are fixed. In this case the first one will be when it gets to the line `*` `Remember to use */ to end this comment`. Here it has no real idea what is going on because the `*/` in this line terminates the comment, and so you've given it a program that starts off with `to end this comment`. In desperation it gives the message `'class' or 'interface' expected` since the program unit should start with one of these. If we remove this line and try again, it highlights the line after the `System.out` call and says `';' expected` because it knows that I forgot the semicolon at the end of the `System.out` statement. If I put one in and compile again, it highlights the `main` method header and says `missing method body, or declare abstract`. This might be harder to work out. The program has a semicolon at the end of this line, which will end the method declaration before it gets to the body, which is the block enclosed between { and }. So as far as it is concerned there is no body. If I remove this extra semicolon and compile again, it next highlights the `System.out` line with the error message `cannot find symbol - method System.out.printline(java.lang.String)`. (`java.lang.String` is the full name of the `String` type). Here I will hopefully notice that the method for `out` should be `println`, not `printline`, fix that, and try again. By now the program has become:

```
/*
 * A program that started with four errors
 */

public class HelloWorld
{
    public static void main()
    {
        System.out.println("Hello World!");
    }
}
```

and to your great relief it finally compiles without any more errors. This is how your programming will usually go; you'll type in your program and expect it to compile. It almost never will. So you keep finding and fixing compile errors until the compiler can't find any more (in the example above there were four), and then you run your program. As you do this, as the example above shows, sometimes the error messages will be very helpful, and in other cases less so; it all depends on how badly you confused the compiler.

4.3 Execution Errors

There are three major kinds of execution errors, infinite loops, abnormal termination errors, and normal termination with incorrect values.

4.3.1 Infinite loops

An infinite loop usually occurs as a result of an error in a loop, so since I haven't introduced loops yet, I'll give an example that should be fairly easy to work through.

Say that I have a code segment:

```
int i = 0;
while (i != 10)
{
    System.out.println(i);
    i += 2;
}
```

There are a couple of new things here. The `while` loop executes the two statements in its block (`System.out.println(i);` and `i += 2;`) as long as `i` is not equal to 10, and `i += 2;` adds 2 to the value of `i`. So this loop will output:

```
2
4
6
8
```

and then stop. So far no problem. Now, however, make one of two changes; either initialize `i` to 1 instead of 0 or leave out the `i += 2;` statement. In the first case `i` will never be equal to 10, and so the segment will output lines containing 1, 3, 5, 7, 9, 11, ... and won't stop for a long time (when `i` gets too big for the computer to store). In the second case the program segment will never stop, and is said to be in an infinite loop, because `i` is always 0 so the segment continuously outputs lines containing just 0. Often an infinite loop won't contain an output, so the program will just appear to be doing nothing and not stopping. In BlueJ when the program is running, you'll see a spinning barber pole symbol in the lower left of the class screen. To stop the execution, and then probably use the debugger described below in Section 4.4, right-click on this symbol and then select `Reset Machine`.

4.3.2 Abnormal termination (throwing an exception)

This happens when Java finds that you are asking it to do something illegal, and it is forced to give up and attempt to tell you what you were asking it to do. This is called *throwing an exception*. In many other languages it is called *raising an exception*.

For example, in my first program I defined the method batAvg() with

```
public double batAvg()
{
    return (double) hits / atBats;
}
```

Say we add a new player to the team and so their hits and atBats fields are both 0. Now we'll attempt to divide zero by zero, and so BlueJ will stop, highlight this statement, and print out the message:

```
ArithmeticException
/ by zero
```

on the bottom of the window. So here the exception being thrown is an arithmetic exception and specifically Java and BlueJ are telling you that you attempted to divide by zero.

As another example, I'll look forward in the book to 1D arrays, which are lists of values. Say that I set up an array named myarray that can store five int values and I then try to access myarray[6].[12] This wil throw ArrayIndexOutOfBoundsException and also tell me that I am attempting to access the element with subscript 6 of the array.

When an exception is thrown and termination is stopped, you have a number of alternatives. First you'll usually try to find out what went wrong by looking at the program code, and fix any problem that you find. This might include using the debugger described in Section 4.4, below. This will be your only option for a while. Another, more advanced option is to catch the exception, which means that you add code that tells Java what to do next; if a specific exception is raised, fix the problem during execution, and then continue. You can even define and throw yur own exceptions. For example, you might have a user-defined exception that is thrown whenever atBats has the value 0 in batAvg(), either output a message or set the batting average to 0.0, and then continue without problems. Exception handling is described in Chapter 18, near the end of this book.

4.3.3 Normal termination with incorrect results

This can either happen because of a typo (as a trivial case, say that you meant to output the value of x but typed System.out.println(y);) or more commonly as a

---

[12] In Java (and other C-like languages) this is the 7th element of the array since its subscripts start at 0, but that doesn't matter here.

result of a logical error when you designed your program. It is often hard to determine where things went wrong, and so unless the error can be found easily, the most common approach is to use the debugger to trace down what went wrong, and where. The debugger is described in the next section.

4.4 The BlueJ Debugger

Debugging is probably the most frustrating part of programming, but fortunately nearly all development environments, including BlueJ, provide tools to make the process less painful. These tools are called debuggers. Debuggers really become useful when your programs include looping statements, and so I will describe the BlueJ debugger in Chapter 11 where loops are introduced.

4.5 Exercises

General questions

1. What is the difference between debugging and testing?

2. Explain in your own words the difference between compile errors and execution errors. Give an example of each.

3. If your program has a compile error, will BlueJ attempt to run the program?

4. If your program has an execution error will BlueJ attempt to run the program? Why?

5. If I have the statement `integer x = 5;` will this be a compile error or an execution error?

In-lab programs

1. There is no formal in-lab for this chapter since no new program design concepts have been introduced.

Out-lab programs

1. There is no formal out-lab for this chapter since no new program design concepts have been introduced.

Chapter 5. Variables and Their Definitions

5.1 Introduction

In the `Player` class I introduced three instance fields, `name`, which held a `String` value and `hits` and `atBats`, both of which held `int` values. They were declared without initial values, and then were initialized in the constructor. In some cases it is better to declare the field with an initial value, which I did in the `UnitTest` class. In some cases we will want to declare variables with initial values, while in other cases we'll want to initialize them later. In particular instance fields are usually initialized in a constructor.

5.2 Declaring Variables

There are two ways to declare a variable,

```
type name;
type name = initial_value;
```

Both ways declare a new variable called `name`, which has the specified type, which could be `int`, `String`, or one of a number of other primitive or derived types that we'll be seeing as the book progresses.

What this means is that we now have a named object[13] that we can use to hold values of the specified type, and then change these values during execution when needed, with the restriction that the new value has the same type, or can be converted by Java to that type.[14]

If the declaration has an initial value component, then it is assigned as the first value of the variable. Obviously this value should also have the same type. So, for example, if we declare:

```
int fred = -30;
```

we will get a new integer variable called `fred` and give it the initial value of `-30`.

If you have to declare, say, five `int` variables `fred`, `jane`, `john`, `jean`, and `susan`, then it gets tedious to have to type:

---

[13] Technically an `int` is not an object, but ignore that for now. This distinction will become important soon, and very important when we get to array lists.

[14] For example, Java can interpret the `int` value 7 as the `double` value 7.0, but cannot interpret any `double` as an `int`.

```
int fred;
int jane;
int john;
int jean;
int susan;
```

and the result is also annoying to read. So Java lets you declare all of them in one line as in:

```
int fred, jane, john, jean, susan;
```

or, which is often better, as:

```
int fred,
    jane,
    john,
    jean,
    susan;
```

If you combine this with an initial value assignment, then you should take some care because Java behaves differently from some other languages. For example, if I say:

```
int x, y = 123;
```

then 123 is only assigned to y in Java, not also to x, which happens in some other languages. So if I now print out the value of x, I'll find that it is undefined.

5.2.1 Commenting variable declarations

When you declare variables, it is excellent practice to get into the habit of describing what they do with a comment, and from now on I'll be doing this. So a typical variable declaration section might be:

```
String first, last;    // user's name
int age = 30,          // user's age
    month, day, year;  // user's date of birth
```

That is, one clumps declarations together as appropriate and adds short comments to make it clear what the variables being declared will be doing. Get into the habit of always doing this and people who have to read your code will greatly appreciate it. I like to line up comments as shown because I think that makes it easier to read, but this is just a personal preference.

5.3 Legal and Appropriate Names for Variables, Methods, and Classes

Names like variable names, method names, and class names are called *identifiers*. The names of identifiers must follow two rules and two conventions. The rules are:

1. An identifier name must be made up of letters (uppercase or lowercase), digits (0, 1, ... 9), underscores (_), and dollar signs ($).
2. The first character in an identifier cannot be a digit.[15]

The two conventions are:

1. Variable and method names always begin with a lowercase letter (a, b, ..., z).
2. Class names always begin with an uppercase letter (A, B, ..., Z).

So the following would be good names for variables or methods:

```
denbigh, susanStarkey, pi, eps358, i, i2j33k, susan_starkey, lots_of_$$
```

The following would be legal names for variables or methods, but would not be appropriate, because they don't follow the first convention:

```
Denbigh, SusanStarkey, PI, EPS358, $$_in_bunches, $100, _poor, MH60S
```

All of the above examples would be legal for class names but only Denbigh, SusanStarkey, PI, EPS358, and MH60S would be appropriate for classes.

The following would **not** be legal names for variables, methods, or classes:

```
358EPS, 358eps, susan-starkey, a_low_%, MH-60S
```

because the first two begin with digits, and – and % are not allowed in identifier names.

5.4 Primitive Data Types

We have already seen variables of type int, which I said could store any integer value. I exaggerated a bit. A variable of type int can actually only store an integer value between about -2.1 billion and +2.1 billion, but this is good enough for most applications.[16] The reason for this restriction is that an int variable is allocated four bytes to store its value, which is 32 bits. This gives 2^{32} possible numbers, which is 4,294,967,296. These are allocated half for negative numbers and half for zero and positive numbers, so the actual range will be -2,147,483,648 to +2,147,483,647, or -2^{31} to +$2^{31} - 1$.

---

[15] Nearly all languages have this restriction because it ensures that you don't try to make a variable name like 3 or 34. If, say, the variable named 3 had the value 7, then Java would have no idea which to print if you tried System.out.println(3);

[16] But not all. For example, as I type this, one site estimates the current world population at 6,774,224,066 people, which couldn't be stored in an int variable. If we wanted to store an estimate of the number of ants in the world, an int wouldn't come close.

int is an example of a primitive data type. Java has eight of these primitive types, so I'll now describe the other seven.

Another important kind of number is the floating point number. This is anything that has a decimal point like 3.14159, -0.33333, 0.0625, or -33.0. The most important type for floating point variables in Java is double, which is given eight bytes, and so can store numbers that can be very big and also very precise. In terms of range of values, double lets you store values between about -10^{308} and $+10^{308}$ with close to 15 significant decimal digits. For example, π can be stored as 3.14159265358979. double values can also be entered using scientific notation, which is mainly used for small or large numbers. For example, -12.34E8 or -12.34e8 is -12.34 times 10^8, which is the double value -1234000000.0 and 1.0E-8 is 0.00000001.

There are some other primitive numeric types that you probably won't use nearly as much as you'll use int and double. Three of these additional types are integer types, and one is floating point:

> byte lets you store integers in one byte, so eight bits. Since 2^8 is 256, this lets you store integer values between -128 and +127.
>
> short lets you store integers in two bytes, so 16 bits. Since 2^{16} is 65,536 this lets you store integer values between -32,768 and +32,767.
>
> long lets you store integers in eight bytes, so 64 bits. Since 2^{64} is about 18.4 quadrillion, this lets you store integer values between about -9 quadrillion and +9 quadrillion.[17] Typically you'll only use long if you really need it, but if, for example, you need your program to store the world's population, which is now estimated at 6,774,432,357, you would use a long to store it since it is too large for an int. You could even store estimates of the number of ants in the world with a long, since there are probably about one quadrillion of them.[18] If long isn't big enough for your numbers, Java has a derived class type called BigInteger where the size of the integer is only limited by your computer's memory, but it is rare to need to use this.[19]
>
> float is the second floating point type. Whereas double uses eight bytes, float only uses four, so its range of possible numbers (approximately -10^{38} to $+10^{38}$) and the precision of those numbers (close to seven decimal digits) is smaller than it is for double. In the past, to save memory space, most programmers used float values nearly all of the time, and only used double

---

[17] If you care, the range is -9,223,372,036,854,775,808 and +9,223,372,036,854,775,807.

[18] Embery, Joan and Ed Lucaire. *Collection of Amazing Animal Facts*. 1983.

[19] NASA scientists estimate that there are about 10^{21} stars in the universe, so that number would require BigInteger. http://imagine.gsfc.nasa.gov/docs/ask_astro/answers/970115.html

values when the extra precision became critical, but now memory is so cheap that using `double` has become the norm in Java. In fact it is inconvenient to use `float` since statements like

```
float x = 3.14;
```

are not allowed because 3.14 is a `double`, which cannot be directly assigned to a lower precision `float` variable. To do this you would have to say:

```
float x = (float) 3.14;
```

which would first cast 3.14 to a `float`. I'll describe this further in the next chapter. Another solution is to use:

```
float x = 3.14f;
```

where the `f` specifies that 3.14 is a float constant.

There are two other primitive data types that are non-numeric:

> `char` lets you store a single character using a system called Unicode, which takes two bytes per character. For example 'D', 'e'. and '@' are single characters. Until recently all systems used only one byte per character, but the reduced price of memory (and hnce its increased size on most systems) has allowed the use of the more complete Unicode system, which includes alternate character sets like Hebrew, Mongolian, and the 85-character Cherokee syllabary. As the examples above show, characters are placed between single quotes to distinguish them from strings. So 's' is a `char` value, "s" is a `string` value.

> `boolean` variables can only have the values `true` or `false`. They use one bit, and store 0 to represent `false` and 1 to represent `true`. So, for example, if we test whether 3 < 7, the result is the `boolean` value `true`.[20]

This completes all of the primitive data types in Java. You might have noticed that `string` hasn't been mentioned. This is because `string` is a derived type built up as a list of individual characters that each have type `char`. As discussed in the last footnote, primitive types begin with a lowercase letter and derived types with an uppercase letter, which is why its name is `String`, not `string`.

---

[20] Usually in mathematics the word Boolean has the uppercase B because it comes from the name of George Boole, but all Java primitive data types begin with a lowercase letter to distinguish them from more complex derived types, which begin with an uppercase letter.

5.5 Scope of Variables

If a variable is declared in a method, then it is said to be local to that method. This means that it exists from the point of declaration to the end of its innermost current block. Within that scope no other variable with the same name can be declared.

Some other languages allow code that is equivalent to the following:

```
// this isn't allowed in Java or C
int i = 8;

for (int i = 0; i < 3; i++)
    System.out.println(i);

System.out.println(i);
```

(I'll be introducing for loops in Chapter 11, but the intent should be obvious) and would output

```
0
1
2
8
```

where one i identifier is allowed in the for loop and another in the outer loop, but in Java the inner i is being declared within the outer block, so this is not allowed.

As an example of where things can go wrong with scoping, consider the following class definition:

```
public class Illegal
{
    private int myInt;

    /* constructor
    public Illegal(int in_myInt)
    {
        myInt = in_myInt;
    }

    public void increasePower()
    {
        myInt *= in_myInt;
    }
}
```

The problem with this is that in_myInt is only defined in the constructor, and its scope ends at the } which terminates that constructor, and so it will be an unknown variable in the increasePower() method.

This is all fairly simple until you get a local variable whose name conflicts with an instance field. This is allowed and is resolved by saying that it is the local variable being referenced when there is an ambiguity. For example, in Chapter 2 I briefly discussed code like:

```
public class Overlap
{
    private int fred;

    // constructor
    public Overlap(int fred)
    {
        fred = fred;
    }

    // methods omitted
}
```

then this is legal, but what is happening in the fred = fred; statement? The parameter fred has scoping precedence over the instance field fred, and so the effect will be that it will be assigned its own value, which doesn't change anything, and in particular the instance field fred hasn't been given a value. A way around this, if you like your instance fields to have the same name as corresponding parameters in constructors, is to use the object named this, which is always defined to the current object. So if you replace fred = fred; in this program with this.fred = fred; then this.fred will refer to the instance field and fred to the constructor parameter, and everything will work well. Personally I don't like using this approach and as you have seen I precede my constructor parameters with in_, but many programmers prefer to use the keyword this.

5.6 Exercises

General questions

1. If you declare a floating point variable in Java, what type are you most likely to use?

2. In addition to the type that you gave in your response to question 1, what other type(s) could be used for a floating point variable?

3. List all floating point types in order of increasing size, and say how many bytes will be assigned to each type.

4. If you declare an integer variable in Java, what type are you most likely to use?

5. In addition to the type that you gave in your response to question 4, what other type(s) could be used for an integer variable?

6. List all integer types in order of increasing sze, and say how many bytes will be assigned to each type.

7. In addition to the floating point and integer types listed above, what are any other primitive types, and how much memory do they need?

8. What is the problem with the declaration `float age = 63.5`?

9. Show three ways to fix the problem with the declaration in Question 8.

10. If I have the declaration `boolean guess;`, what values can be assigned to `guess`?

11. Why does Java use `String` as the name of the type for string variables and not `string`?

12. Which of the following would be a legal name for a variable?
`Denbigh, denbigh, $5, $_$, $-$, 357EPS, EPS357, DStarkey, D_Starkey, dStarkey, d_starkey`?

13. Which of the following would be a good name for a variable?
`Denbigh, denbigh, $5, $_$, $-$, 357EPS, EPS357, DStarkey, D_Starkey, dStarkey, d_starkey`?

14. Which of the following would be a legal name for a class?
`Denbigh, denbigh, $5, $_$, $-$, 357EPS, EPS357, DStarkey, D_Starkey, dStarkey, d_starkey`?

15. Which of the following would be a good name for a class?
`Denbigh, denbigh, $5, $_$, $-$, 357EPS, EPS357, DStarkey, D_Starkey, dStarkey, d_starkey`?

16. Why doesn't Java let you include a period in an identifier name? For example, why isn't `a.b` allowed as a variable name?

17. Why doesn't Java let you begin an identifier name with a digit?

18. Java has a built-in class called `Integer` that includes a predefined constant, `Integer.MIN_VALUE`, which is the most negative value that you can store in an `int` variable. That is, it contains -2^{31}. What will happen if you attempt the assignment `big = -Integer.MIN_VALUE;`?

19. Is the declaration `boolean b = 1;` legal? Why, or why not?

20. Find all of the errors in the following code segment:

```
int x = 3;
int y = -5.0,
string s$t = 'abc';
Boolean b.c = true;
        d = "false";
```

In-lab programs

1. In the game of cricket one keeps statistics on two kinds of players, batsmen (similar to hitters in baseball) and bowlers (similar to pitchers). Create a class called Batsman that has six instance fields, name (String), innings (int), notOut (int), runs (int), highScore (int), and ballsFaced (int). The class will have a constructor that has six parameters to set these values for a Batsman. There will be two methods: (a) double average() computes the player's batting average, which is their runs divided by their number of completed innings, which is innings - notOut. E.g., if a player has had 97 innings and was not out 4 times, then their completed innings is 93. (Remember to avoid the int divide problem throughout this assignment.) (b) double scoringRate() is computed as (runs / ballsFaced) * 100. For example, if you have Batsman kp = new Batsman("Kevin Petersen", 97, 4, 4647, 226, 7404); then kp.average() should be about 49.97 (from 4647 / (93 - 4)), and kp.scoringRate() should be about 62.76 (from (4647 / 7404) * 100).[21]

Out-lab programs

1. Add two methods to your Batsman class from in-lab 1, String getName() returns the batsman's name and int getHS() returns their high score.

2. Add a new class, Bowler, which has five instance fields, firstName (String), lastName (String), ballsBowled (int), runs (int), and wickets (int). The class will have a constructor that has five parameters to set these values for a Bowler. There will be three methods: (a) double average() computes the player's bowling average, which is their runs divided by their number of wickets, (b) double economy() is computed as (runs / ballsBowled) * 6,

---

[21] See http://www.cricinfo.com/ci/content/player/19296.html for KP's page. Statistics on more players are at http://www.cricinfo.com/ci/content/current/player/index.html

and (c) `String getName()` will return the full name of the `Bowler`. For example, `kp.getName()` will return "`Kevin Petersen`". Note the space in the middle. To do this you'll use the + concatenation operator twice. For example, if we have `Bowler kp = new Bowler("Kevin", "Petersen", 735, 518, 4);` then `kp.average()` should be about `129.50` and `kp.economy()` should be about `4.23`. Implement the class and write a JUnit class to test it using the data on KP shown above.

3. Write a class for a `main` method which has two additional `void` methods called `batInfo()` and `bowlInfo()`, which print out nicely formatted information on a player. For technical reasons, which shouldn't concern you yet, the methods will have to be declared `static`, as shown. Specifically, the class should be (I've removed most comments and some code):

```
/**
 * Cricket main class for lab 3
 * @author Denbigh Starkey
 * @version 9/14/09
 */
public class Cricket
{
    public static void batInfo(Batsman batsman)
    {
        // you'll need code consisting of print and printlns here
    }

    public static void bowlInfo(Bowler bowler)
    {
        // you'll need code consisting of print and printlns here
    }

    public static void main()
    {
        Batsman kpBat = new Batsman("Kevin Petersen", 97, 4, 4647,
                                226, 7404);
        Bowler kpBowl = new Bowler("Kevin", "Petersen", 735, 518, 4),
                monty = new Bowler("Mudhsuden", "Panesar", 9042, 4331, 126);

        batInfo(kpBat);
        bowlInfo(kpBowl);
        bowlinfo(monty);
    }
}
```

Then output, for the example above, should be:

```
Kevin Petersen's batting stats:
    Batting average: 49.96774193548387
    Scoring rate:    62.763371150729334
    High Score:      226 runs

Kevin Petersen's bowling stats:
    Bowling average: 129.5
    Bowling economy: 4.228571428571429

Mudhsuden Panesar's bowling stats:
    Bowling average: 34.37301587301587
    Bowling economy: 2.873921698739217
```

Chapter 6. Assignment Statements and Expressions

6.1 Introduction

One of the strengths of a computer is that it can perform complex arithmetic and string operations extremely fast and very accurately. To do these operations we need to be able to specify the operations that we want to perform through arithmetic expressions and string expressions, and then save the resuts somewhere through assignment statements so that the results can be reused in subsequent expresions or output in reports.

Java also has a number of built-in methods that perform common arithmetic and string procedures. For example, it is common to need to compute the square root or the cube root of a number or to compute x^y for values x and y, and so instead of forcing everyone to write their own methods for these common operations Java provides them through methods called `sqrt()`, `cbrt()`, and `pow()` in a built-in class called `Math`. Similarly a `string` class provides many common string operations.

6.2 Assignment Statements

When I introduced declarations with initial values, I showed one way to assign a value to a variable. So, for example,

```
int hastingsBattle = 1066;
```

creates an integer variable called `hastingsBattle` and gives it the value 1066. Usually variable values are initialized during execution and then often change through *assignment statements*.

An assignment statement has the syntax

```
variable = newvalue;
```

which will change the value of the variable to `newvalue`, which obviously must have the appropriate type. For example,

```
int jane;
jane = 5;
```

is equivalent to

```
int jane = 5;
```

There wouldn't be that much point in having assignment statements if that is all that they did, but in fact they are much more powerful than this example shows. The value on the right side of the = in the assignment will, for now, be an arithmetic or string expression, so we'll go ahead and look at what they are.

6.3 Arithmetic Expressions

Say that I have two variables representing my height in feet and meters, then once I've calculated my height in feet I'd like to use the statement

```
meters = feet * 0.3048;
```

to calculate the correct value for my height in meters. For example, consider the Java program below:

```
/*
 * Given my height in feet, compute my height in meters.
 * Author: Denbigh Starkey
 */
public class TestIt
{
    public static void main()
    {
        double feet = 6.292,   // my height in feet
               meters;         // my height in meters
        meters = 0.3048 * feet;
        System.out.println("Height is " + feet + "' or " + meters + "m");
    }
}
```

When I run this program, it gives me the output:

```
Height is 6.292' or 1.9178016m
```

What I have done here is to assign the value of an arithmetic expression, 0.3048 * feet, as the new value of the variable meters, and this has let me do something useful. Note that I'm using * to multiply two values, so we say that * is the multiplication operator.

Java has many kinds of expressions like, say, Boolean expressions, but in this section I'll just look at arithmetic expressions.

Ignore one detail at this point, which is the output value for my height in meters. Clearly Java has output the value to an absurd level of precision, and we'd probably prefer to get a value like 1.92, because the digits after that are meaningless, but I'll hold off showing how to take control of your output precision until Chapter 10.[22]

When looking at arithmetic expressions, some of the questions that need answering are what arithmetic operators exist in Java, how do they work with the different primitive numeric data types, and what happens if we mix data types in an expression. Also, what happens if, for example, we use an assignment statement to try to assign a `double` value arithmetic expression to an `int` variable? There are some nasty little details in here, so pay attention to them.

6.3.1 Arithmetic operators

Java has five binary[23] operators that work on numbers, +,-, *, /, and %.

For all of the operators, if both of the arguments have an integer type (`byte`, `short`, `int`, or `long`), then the result will be an integer type, but if at least one of the arguments has a floating point type (`float` or `double`), the result will be a floating point type. The particular type of integer or floating point result will be based on the most complicated of the arguments. So, for example, if a `long` is added to a `float`, then the result must be a floating point type, and since the most complex floating point type here is `float`, that will be the result. The following table gives results for all possible combinations:

	byte	short	int	long	float	double
byte	byte	short	int	long	float	double
short	short	short	int	long	float	double
int	int	int	int	long	float	double
long	long	long	long	long	float	double
float	float	float	float	float	float	double
double	double	double	double	double	double	double

For example, if the arguments to a numerical operator are `float` and `double`, the result is `double`, and if they are `byte` and `long`, the result is `long`.

Now I'll look at the five binary arithmetic operations in more detail:

+ is addition. For example, 3 + 7 is 10, 3 + 7.0 is 10.0, and 1.1 + 11.1 is 12.2.

---

[22] If this delay annoys you, the solution is to replace the output statement with a single statement: `System.out.printf("Height is %.3f' or %.2fm%n", feet, meters);` which will output `Height is 6.292' or 1.92m`. Look ahead to Chapter 10 (Input/Output) if you want to get ahead on this, but there is no need to do that.

[23] A binary operator has two arguments, as compared to a unary operator, which has only one argument.

- is subtraction. For example, 3 - 7 `is` -4, 3 - 7.0 is -4.0, and 1.1 - 11.1 is -10.0.

* is multiplication. Java, like most other languages, uses * instead of the more traditional mathematical operator × for multiplication. So, for example, 3 * 7 is 21, 3 * 7.0 is 21.0, and 1.1 * 11.1 is 12.21.

/ is division. Java (and most other languages) uses / instead of the more traditional mathematical operator ÷ for division. For example, 7 / 4 is 1, 7 / 4.0 is 1.75, and 7.0 / 2.0 is 3.5. The one that might be surprising here is 7 / 4; since both arguments are integer, the rules say that the result must be integer, and the result is computed by throwing away the fractional part. Consider the test program:

```
/**
 * Check a few integer divides
 * Author: Denbigh Starkey
 */
public class TestIt
{
    public static void main()
    {
        System.out.println(7 / 4);
        System.out.println(-7 / 4);
        System.out.println(5 / 4);
        System.out.println(-5 / 4);
    }
}
```

The output will be

```
1
-1
1
-1
```

So with integer division, the result isn't rounded to the nearest integer, but instead the fractional part is discarded, however big it is. You have to be careful with this; for example, many people get surprised when they find that 2 / 3 is 0. To get the expected results, make at least one of them a double as in 2.0 / 3, 2 / 3.0, or 2.0 / 3.0.

The final arithmetic operator is %, which gives you the remainder when you do a divide. So, for example, 7 % 4 is 3 and -7 % 4 is -3. This is almost always used with integer arguments, and so then the result will be integer. However in Java it is also defined for floating point numbers or mixed expressions.[24] For example, 7 % 1.6 is 0.6, which is the remainder when 1.6 is divided into 7. Most programmers only use this operator with integer arguments, and in this book I will make that restriction.

---

[24] This is a place where Java is different from C,/C++ where % can only be used with integer arguments.

As I've shown above, - can also be used as a unary operator in front of a number to change its sign. + can also be used as a unary operator, but it doesn't do anything useful. Java permits expressions like 9 - -4 or even 9- -4, giving 13 for both, but if you were to try 9--4 it would fail because, as we'll see in Section 6.3.3, -- is a Java unary operator and so it gets confused. Most languages don't allow two consecutive operators, and it is a good rule, even if you are programming in Java, to avoid them, so 9 - (-4) would be a much better way to write the expression.

6.3.2 Operator precedence

We can combine arithmetic operators when building expressions, and use parentheses to group things together, and so typical arithmetic expressions are:

```
a * b + c * d
a * (b + c) * d
a / b * c
-a * -b + -c
a - b - c
```

The question is how should they be interpreted? That is, in what order should we evaluate the pieces of the expression? The rules are:

1. Expressions inside parentheses are evaluated first.
2. Unary + and - have the highest precedence and so are performed before other operators.
3. *, /. and % have the next highest precedence and so are performed next.
4. Binary + and - have lowest precedence and so are performed last.
5. If you have to choose between two operators with equal precedence (e.g. * and % or * and *) the evaluation is done left to right.

Following these rules the expressions above are equivalent to the fully parenthesized expressions:

```
((a * b) + (c * d))
((a * (b + c)) * d)
((a / b) * c)
(((-a) * (-b)) + (-c))
((a - b) - c)
```

Most of these follow your normal mathematical expectations. The only one that might be a concern is the third example. For example, many people expect 12 / 2 * 3 to have the value 2, but it will be 18.[25]

---

[25] For completely different reasons in both APL and SNOBOL the value of this expression would be 2, but most languages would give it the same value that Java does, namely 18.

If you are concerned that your code isn't easy to read, then use parenthesis to clarify what you are doing.

6.3.3 Increment and decrement operators (++ and --)

It is common to want to add one to a variable or subtract one from a variable. In Java this is done with the ++ and -- operators. These operators can be put either in front of or behind the argument, with subtle timing differences in meaning, but initially I'll just look at when they follow their argument.

If we use, say, x++ in an arithmetic expression, then two things happen; its value for the expression will be the value of x, but it will then increase x's value by one. For example, say we have the following Java program:

```
public class TestIt
{
    public static void main()
    {
        int x = 5;
        System.out.println(2 * x++);
        System.out.println(x);
    }
}
```

The values printed out will be 10 and 6. So the current value of x (which is 5) will be used in the expression and then x's value will be incremented (increased by one). If the code had contained x-- instead of x++, the values printed would have been 10 and 4.

If we use ++ or -- in front of a variable then the timing is altered; first the variable is incremented or decremented, and then that changed value becomes the value used in the expression. For example, if we change the program to

```
public class TestIt
{
    public static void main()
    {
        int x = 5;
        System.out.println(2 * ++x);
        System.out.println(x);
    }
}
```

then the values output will be 12 and 6. If we used --x instead of ++x, the values would be 8 and 4.

The thing to remember is that if the order is ++variable or -variable, then the increment or decrement is done before we evaluate the variable, but if it is variable++ or variable--, then we evaluate the variable first and then increment or decrement it.

++ or -- should only be used with variables, not with expressions. For example, the expression --(3 + x) is an error.

The most common use of ++ (or --) is not in a complex arithmetic expression, but is by itself with a variable in an expression. E.g., instead of writing

```
x = x + 1;
y = y - 1;
```

it is normal style to use

```
x++;
y--;
```

which are equivalent, so you should use the short form in this situation.

My main advice is to keep things relatively simple and not use ++ and -- too much in expressions. It is easy to get carried away and produce unreadable code. For example, if you have the statement

```
z = ++x + --y;
```

it is fancy and clever, but the longer replacement code

```
z = x + y;
x++;
y--;
```

is much clearer and is preferred. The problem with the one-line version is that you have to think before you work out that the expression will increment x and decrement y before the pieces of the expression are evaluated, so in effect it will evaluate to (x + 1) + (y - 1), which is just x + y, whereas you don't need to think when evaluating the three-line alternative.

If you insist on using a one-line version, then

```
z = x++ + y--;
```

would be a bit clearer than the original one-liner, and is equivalent to it, but it is still not nearly as good as the three-liner.

6.4 String Expressions

Java's String class includes a concatenation operator, +., which I first showed in println() calls. Concatenation[26] joins two strings together, and so, for example,

---

[26] Catena is the Latin for chain, so concatenation means chaining things together.

"First Half" + "Second Half" has the value "First HalfSecond Half". The concatenation operator will also convert other types to strings, and so, for example, the statement

```
int x = -33;
System.out.println("The value of x is " + x);
```

will output

```
The value of x is -33
```

This is obviously much nicer than using:

```
int x = -33;
System.out.print("The value of x is ");
System.out.println(x);
```

Output statements like this are where the concatenation operator (+) is most commonly used. However the need for it becomes much less when formatted output is used. I'll introduce this in Chapter 10.

The + can look weird when numbers are involved. However, if Java sees it where one of the arguments is a string, it will interpret it as concatenation not addition. If both arguments are numeric, then it will be interpreted as addition. For example,

```
System.out.println(3 + 4);
System.out.println(3 + "4");
```

will interpret the first as addition and the second as concatenation and will output

```
7
34
```

6.5 Back to Assignment Statements

In this section I'll just describe arithmetic assignment statements. An assignment statement, as we have seen, usually has the form

```
variable = expression;
```

The expression is evaluated and then that value becomes the new value of the variable. So, for example,

```
int x = 5;
x = 2 * x - 3;
System.out.println(x);
```

will output 7.

So far this is easy. The problem comes if the left and right hand sides of the assignment statements have different types. For example,

```
double x;
x = 3 / 4;
System.out.println(x);
```

The programmer is probably hoping that x will get the value 0.75 and that this will be output, but 3 / 4 is a divide with two integer arguments, and so it gives the integer result 0, which is then to be assigned to x. Since x is a double it converts 0 to 0.0, and that becomes the value of x that is output.

That is, first the expression is evaluated ignoring the variable on the left-hand side, and then if both sides have the same type, the assignment will be made. If the types are different, then it will convert the right-hand side to the left-hand side type if it can be done without problems.

The kinds of assignments that are allowed are:

integer_type = same_or_shorter_integer_type;
float_type = float or integer_type;
double = anything;

Anything else will be blocked. For example, all of the following will be legal:

```
float x;        double x;        int x;
int y = 7;      float y = 7.3;   short y;
x = y;          x = y;           x = y;
```

but the following will not be allowed:

```
float x;        double x;        int x;
int y = 7;      float y = 7.3;   short y;
y = x;          y = x;           y = x;
```

6.5.1 Type casting

Say that we have:

```
double x = 10.0, y = 3.5;
int z;
z = x * y;
```

This will be blocked because we are trying to assign a double to an int. However, obviously we'd like to be able to do something like this and finish up with z containing 35. To make this possible Java provides *casting functions* for all of the standard types, which have the form (newtype) and convert whatever follows into that type. For example,

```
public class TestIt
{
    public static void main()
    {
        double x = 10, y = 3.5;
        int z;
        z = (int) (x * y);
        System.out.println("z = " + z);
    }
}
```

shows the use of casting to an int. The cast (int) expression converts the floating point expression to an int, throwing away any decimal part if there is one. So this program will compute the double 35.0, then convert that to the integer value 35, which will then be output. If y's initialization had been 3.57 instead of 3.5, then 35 would still have been output because 10 * 3.57 is 35.7 and (int) 35.7 is 35.

Let's return to a previous problem. Say one has:

```
int x = 3, y = 4;
double z;
z = x / y;
```

As discussed earlier, z will get the value 0.0 because of the integer divide. It won't help to convert the assignment to

```
z = (double) (x / y);
```

because x / y is still 0 and (double) 0 is still 0.0. The solution is to convert either x's or y's value to a double (or both) and then do the divide, which will then have a double result. For example, replace the assignment statement with

```
z = ((double) x) / y;
```

and now it will output 0.75. We can simplify this because casts attach to the nearest thing, so we could write the statement as

```
z = (double) x / y;
```

which is equivalent.

6.6 +=, -=, *=. /=, %=

Java has a convenient shorthand for assignments of the form

```
variable = variable operator value;
```

which is

```
variable operator= value;
```

As an example, instead of saying

```
x = x + 7;
```

we can just write

```
x += 7;
```

this not only looks cleaner, but also makes it easier for the compiler to be efficient in some cases. It works for all of our operators and so, for example,

```
int x = 14,
    y = 3;
x %= y;
```

is equivalent to

```
int x = 14,
    y = 3;
x = x % y;
```

and it will assign 2 to x.

6.7 Assignment Statements with Objects

As we have seen, there are eight primitive types, the six numeric types, char, and boolean. Values in these types are not objects, but anything else that you'll be dealing with is an object.

If x and y are declared to be from a primitive type and we execute

```
x = y;
```

then y's value is copied in to x. For example, say we have:

```
int x, y;
y = 5;
x = y;
System.out.println("x = " + x + ",  y = " + y);
y += 3;
System.out.println("x = " + x + ",  y = " + y);
```

then the output will be

```
x = 5, y = 5
x = 5, y = 8
```

So when y changes, that doesn't affect x's value.

When a similar assignment is made with objects that are instances of a class, then there is a big difference. The value of an object is a reference to where it is in memory, and so if x and y are both instances of a Player object, then their values are the same block of memory. Now, say, we have a method that changes y's number of at bats, the effect will be to also change x's number of at bats, which probably isn't what was wanted. To get round, this Java has a method called clone(), which makes a copy of an object, but I won't get into how to use it here. For now the easiest approach is to just copy the individual components of one object into the other.

6.8 Built-in Arithmetic Methods

In addition to its arithmetic expression operators, Java also has a number of useful methods that operate on numbers. These methods are collected into a Java class called Math.[27] This provides common mathematical methods including abs() (absolute value), sin(), asin(), sinh(), and similar cos and tan methods, sqrt() and cbrt() (cube root), exp(), log(), and log10(), max() and min(), and pow (pow(a, b) returns the value of a^b), plus many more. Some of these methods expect one argument (e.g., one can compute Math.abs(-7.3)) and some two (e.g., Math.max(7.5, 3.7) returns 7.5).

There is redundancy in some of these methods. E.g. to get the cube root of 7.4 one could use cbrt(7.4) or pow(7.4, 1.0 / 3.0).

To call these methods you must specify that they are in the Math class, and so, for example, to assign the value of the product of the square root of 7.3 and the sine of 0.3 to a variable x you would use:

```
x = Math.sqrt(7.3) * Math.sin(0.3);
```

Since these methods are operating on numerical primitive types, not on objects, the methods in the Math class are all static.

Math also includes two public field constants, E and PI, which give the values of e and π respectively. For example, to find the area of a circle given its radius use:

```
area = Math.PI * radius * radius;
```

---

[27] There is another class called strictMath that ensures identical results on different systems, but Math methods have more efficient implementations, so it is usually used.

6.9 Built-in String Methods

Built-in methods for processing strings are in the String class. However, they are called very differently from the way in which arithmetic methods are called. This is because strings are objects, unlike the eight intrinsic types that include the six numeric types. So say that I have the declaration:

```
String name = "Denbigh Starkey";
```

and I want to print out name's length. There is a method in the String class, length(), which does this, but I have to apply it to name, which is a String object. That is, I cannot use length(name) but instead I use name.length(). Any String valued object can be used where I have name in this expression. For example, the following code, where I first use a variable and then use a String constant, will output 5 7. (Remember that + concatenates strings.)

```
String first = "Susan";
System.out.println(first.length() + " " + "Starkey".length());
```

Some of the many other methods in the String class are:

- compareTo() lexicographically compares the object against another string
- concat() concatenates (links together) the two strings.
- contains() checks whether the formal parameter string or character is a substring of the object string.
- endsWith() and startsWith() determine whether the actual parameter is a suffix or prefix of the object string.
- indexOf() determines whether the actual parameter is a substring of the object and if so where it begins.
- replace() replaces occurrences of its first actual parameter with the first.
- substring() returns a specified substring of the object string.
- toUpperCase() and toLowerCase() convert the string to upper or lower case..

Say name contains "Denbigh Starkey" and one computes name.indexOf("gh");. This will return 5. If instead of "gh" I used 'D' it would return 0 to show that it is at the beginning of the string, and if I tried "x" it would return -1 to show that the string is not a substring of the object. Note that the first letter of the string is in position 0, not 1.

A common mistake is to assume that replace() forms a replacement in the object string, but all String methods are immutable, which means that they don't change their object. So, for example, if name contains "Denbigh Starkey" then

69

```
String daughter = name.replace("Denbigh", "Susan");
```

assigns "Susan Starkey" to daughter but leaves name containing "Denbigh Starkey". The common error is that if I were to just try the statement:

```
name.replace("Denbigh", "Susan");
```

then it will do nothing because the result needs to be assigned somewhere.

As another example that uses two of the String methods, consider the code:

```
String name = "Susan Starkey";
spaceSpot = name.indexOf(" ");          // spaceSpot is 5
first = name.substring(0, spaceSpot);   // first five characters of name
last = name.substring(spaceSpot + 1);   // rest of name starting at 6th
```

name.indexOf(" ") finds the position of the first space in name, as discussed above. When substring() has two parameters, for example name.substring(a, b), it returns the substring of name starting at position a that has length (b - a). When it has one parameter, as in name.substring(a), it returns the remainder of name, starting at position a. I've used both versions here.

In Chapter 8 I'll show how to use Java's online documentation to look at built-in classes like the String class, so that you can see details on how all of the methods work.

6.10 Accessor and Mutator Methods

An important technical point is that all of the methods in the String class are *immutable.* This means that none of them alter the String object that they are applied to. If all of the methods in a class are immutable (cannot change instances of the class), then the class is also said to be immutable, so String is an immutable class and String objects are immutable objects.

Java classifies methods on how they affect the objects that they manipulate. These definitions then extend into some classes that contain methods.

The simplest definitions are those for *mutator* methods and *accessor* methods. If a method just accesses the values in an object without changing them, then it is called an accessor method. If, however, it can change the object, then it is called a mutator method. So an accessor method just accesses its object without changing it while a mutator method changes (mutates) its object. By changing an object I mean that its instance fields are changed, because these are what describe the state of an object.

70

Consider the Player class from Chapter 2. The methods that return a player's stats is an accessor because it doesn't change the stats, whereas a method that updates the player's at bat and hit counts is a mutator.

6.11 Exercises

General questions

1. Is the `Player` class defined in Chapter 2 an immutable class? Explain.

2. If I added two methods to the `Player` class in Chapter 2 called `addHits()` and `addAtBats()`, which let you update a player's hits and at bats after a game, would the `Player` class be an immutabable class? Explain.

3. If I have two string variables `first` and `last` that contain a person's first and last names, how can I use the + operator to assign the full name (including a space in the middle) to the variable `name`? For example, if I assign `first` = "Denbigh; and `last` = "Starkey"; the new statement should assign "Denbigh Starkey" to `name`.

4. Repeat the last question but use the `concat()` method instead of the + operator.

5. What will be output by `System.out.println(2 + 6 + "8");`?

6. What will be output by `System.out.println("2" + 6 + 8);`?

7. After executing the following statements, what will be the values of x and y?

```
int x = 7,
    y = 5;
x = y;
y = x;
```

8. If, in the last question, I'd left off the last statement (`y = x;`), what difference, if any, would that have made to the answer to the question?

9. For each of the following code segments, say whether it is legal or illegal in Java. If it is illegal give a brief reason.

```
int x = 7;          int x = 7;          int x = 7;
double y = 3.0;     double y = 3.0;     double y = 3;
x = y * 4;          y = x * 4;          y = x * 4.0;
```

10. Fully parenthesize the following expressions to show their evaluation order.

```
a + b * c / e * f
a * b + c * d
a - b + c
```

11. What are the values of the following expressions? Show double results with a decimal point, int results without a decimal point.

```
3 + 2.0 * 4 - 1
7 / 2 * 5
7 / 2 * 5.0
7.0 / 2 * 5
6 / 2 + 4
```

12. What will be output by the following code segment?

```
String course = "CS160";
course.replace("160", "215");
System.out.println(course);
```

13. What will be output by the following code segment?

```
String course = "CS160",
       otherCourse;
otherCourse = course.replace("160", "215");
System.out.println(course);
```

14. What will be output by the following statements?

```
System.out.println(44 + 33);
System.out.println(44 + "33");
System.out.println("44" + 33);
System.out.println("44" + "33");
```

15. What will be output by the following statements? Include a decimal point only if the result is double.

```
System.out.println(11 / 2 * 3);
System.out.println(11 / 2.0 * 3);
System.out.println(11 / 2 * 3.0);
System.out.println(11 % 2 * 3.0);
System.out.println(11 % 2 * 3);
```

In-lab programs

1. A person's body mass index is defined as their weight in pounds times 703 divided by the square of their height in inches. Implement a class called Healthy which has two instance fields, height and weight, both int values, a

single constructor which sets these values, and a method called `myBMI()` that returns a double using the expression described above.

2. In Chapter 5, out-lab 3, you developed two methods called `batInfo(Batsman batsman)` and `bowlInfo(Bowler bowler)`. Move these into the `Cricket` class so that they will give the same output as before. They will now be `batInfo()` and `bowlInfo()`.

Out-lab programs

1. Add a method to the `Batsman` class, `public String getFirstName()`, which uses the `indexOf()` and `substring()` methods in the `String` class to return the first name of the Batsman. Use `indexOf()` to find the location of the first space in the name and then `substring()` to extract the first part of the string up to the position specified by the `indexOf()` result.

2. Design and implement a class called `radiusStuff` that has one instance field, `double radius`, and three methods: `diameter()` returns the diameter of the circle with that radius, `circumference()` returns the circumference computed as π times the diameter, and `volume()` returns the volume of the sphere with that radius. Note that when computing the circumference you shoul use your `diameter()` method, not use 2 times π times the radius. This is to show that one method can call on another. Test your class using both a JUnit class and also a class named MainTest the contains a `main()` method.

3. Add another method to `radiusStuff`, `double yOnCircle(double x)` which, given a value for x, will return a y value where the point (x, y) lies on the circle centered at the origin with the given radius. Use the expression `Math.sqrt(r * r - x * x)` to get the value. For example, if `radius` is 5 then `yOnCircle(3.0)` wil return `4.0`. Add this to your two test classes.

4. Add another method `zOnSphere(double x, double y)`, that finds the z value of a point (x, y, z) on the sphere centered at the origin with the specified radius.

Chapter 7. Extending the Player Class

7.1 Introduction

In Chapter 2 I introduced the Player class as my first Java program. In this chapter I'll extend the class to make it more useful and use the extensions to get into the heart of Java and Object-Oriented Programming and Design (OOP and OOD), which is objects.

The major additions that I will make to the Player project are:

- Add a variable to the Player class that keeps track of how many Player class objects have been created.
- Add a new class called Stats that will save the number of hits and at bats for a player.
- Add a method in the Player class that returns a Stats object that contains two values, the player's number of hits and at bats.
- Add a new unit test class that tests these features.

7.2 The Three New Classes

7.2.1 The JUnit Test class

```java
public void testPlayer()
{
    Player greatOne = new Player("Mick Jagger", 245, 300),
           jack = new Player("John Adams", 30, 300);
    assertEquals(Player.teamSize(), 2);

    Player ringo = new Player("Richard Starkey", 27, 120);
    assertEquals(Player.teamSize(), 3);

    assertEquals(jack.batAvg(), 0.100, 0.001);
    Stats jackStats = jack.getStats();
    assertEquals(jackStats.getAtBats(), 300);
}
```

I've started with the JUnit test class because it shows the capabilities that I want in this program. Usually this class would test far more, but I want to keep it simple here.

I've created two new objects of class Player named greatOne and jack. I then check to make sure that the team size is 2. When I add a third player, ringo, the team size is three. So keeping track of the number of objects that have been created is

75

working. The next line checks jack's batting average using the batAvg() method from the Player class, with a tolerance of 0.001. Finally I use a new method from Player, getStats(), to return a pair containing jack's number of hits and at bats, and then use a method from the Stats class, getAtbats(), to return the number of at bats from this Stats pair.

Now I'll look at the two classes that do this, Stats and Player. I'll start with the Stats class.

7.2.3 The Stats class

In the description, above, I said that I want the method, getStats(), to return a pair of values. However a method call will either be declared as void, which means that it returns no values, or as having a type, which means that it returns a single object or value of that type. So to return a pair of values I'm going to create a new class called Stats whose instanced objects contain the pair of values that I need, and then in Player I can have a method that returns one of these Stats objects.

This might seem to be new, but consider getname() which returned a String. A String is actually a complex object built up out of a collection of char values, so in many ways it is more complex than returning a Stats pair.

There isn't anything very complex going on in Stats. It has two private instance fields, hits and atBats, and then two methods that give public access to these values. This is typical for a class whose only goal is to provide a mechanism for storing a structure that is more complex than a single value.

```
public class Stats
{
    private int hits,
               atBats;

    public Stats(int in_hits, int in_atBats)
    {
        // initialize instance fields
        hits = in_hits;
        atBats = in_atBats;
    }

    public int getHits()
    {
        return hits;
    }

    public int getAtBats()
    {
        return atBats;
    }
}
```

7.2.3 The New Player class

The code for this is shown below. The instance fields and the batAvg() method are unchanged from my first example in Chapter 2, I've added a method getName() as discussed there, and the constructor has only a small change, so I'll concentrate on the differences described on the last page.

The new method getStats() should return two values, the player's number of hits and number of at bats. As discussed above, I'm going to return a single object that is an instance of the Stats class that contains two values in its instance fields. In the method I create a new local Stats object called newStats with

```
Stats newStats = new Stats(hits, atBats);
```

following the same format that I used for creating Player objects, and return it.

```java
public class Player
{
    // instance fields
    private String name;
    private int hits,
                atBats;

    // class fields
    private static int numPlayers = 0;

    public Player(String in_name, int in_hits, int in_atBats)
    {
        name = in_name;
        hits = in_hits;
        atBats = in_atBats;
        numPlayers++;
    }

    public double batAvg()
    {
        return (double) hits / atBats;
    }

    public String getName()
    {
        return name;
    }

    public Stats getStats()
    {
        Stats newStats = new Stats(hits, atBats);
        return newStats;
    }

    public static int teamSize()
    {
        return numPlayers;
    }
}
```

The most significant addition here, apart from the use of the new `Stats` class, is that I am now keeping track of the number of `Player` objects that I have created. To do this there are three new additions, a variable called `NumPlayers`, an addition to the constructor, and a new method called `teamsize()`, which returns the number of players.

`numPlayers` is declared below the instance fields with the declaration:

```
private static int numPlayers = 0;
```

Note the keyword `static`. Instance fields like `hits` are created for each `Player` object (instance), and so, for example, `jack` and `greatOne` will each have their own `atBats` value. However, `numPlayers`, which I want to keep track of the number of `Player` objects created, is a property of the `Player` class, not of individual players. Earlier I used the keyword `static` to refer to methods (e.g., `main()`), which didn't operate on individual objects. The use here is similar; since it operates on the class and not on objects/instances from the class. It is called a *class field*, *class variable*, *static field*, or *static variable*, and is designated with the keyword `static`.

I need to initialize `numPlayers` to 0 when the class is created since there aren't any `Player` objects that have been instanced yet. Whenever a new `Player` object is created, it is through a call to the `Player` constructor, and so to keep count of the number of players I just need to add one to `numPlayers` with `numPlayers++;` in the constructor, as shown.

The new method `teamSize()` gives `public` access to the value of the `private` class field `numPlayers`. Since it isn't an operation on an object but on a class field it must be declared as a `static` method as shown.

7.3 Instance Fields *vs.* Class Fields

In the `Player` class I used three instance fields and one class field. It is important to understand the difference between them.

If an instance field is declared in a class, then every instance (object) of the class will have its own independent copy of the field. For example, every `Player` object has its own value for its name. If a class field is declared, then only one copy of that field will exist, and its goal will be to provide information about the class. For example, in the example in this chapter the field kept track of how many objects had been created in the class.

As another example of a class field, say that I want to compute the team's batting average. To do this I need to know the total of all of the players' hits and at bats, which I can store as two class fields, teamHits and teamAtBats. Both of these would be initialized to zero, and whenever a player was added through a constructor call, I would add the new hits and at bats values to these class fields.

Another critical difference between instance fields and class fields is where they are initialized. Instance fields will usually be initialized in the constructor call, and in fact this is the primary goal of the constructor. Class fields, however, can't be initialized in the constructor, because that would mean that they are reinitialized every time a new object is created. So class fields are usually initialized when they are declared. Look again at the Player class; numPlayers is initialized to zero when it is declared, but there are no initializations in the declarations of name, hits, and atBats – they are initialized in the constructor.

7.4 The Class Diagram

The UnitTest class uses methods from both Player and Stats, and the Player class uses a Stats object. When I go to the class diagram and hit the compile button it compiles all three classes and shows these connections with arrows. The class diagram now looks like:

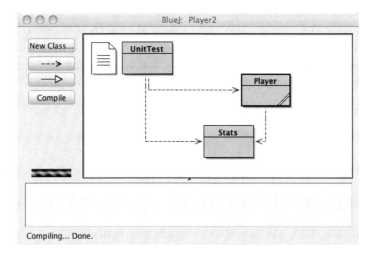

I've dragged the three classes around a bit to make the picture look a bit better.

7.5 Coupling

When you design a program with multiple classes under BlueJ, it automatically generates a class diagram that shows the dependencies between the classes as arrows. If a class depends on another class, then if modifications are made to the methods or constructors in the second class, then you'll also have to see whether you need to make corresponding changes to the dependent class. If you get too many dependencies, then the problem with updates requiring changes to other classes gets out of hand. For example, I wrote an artificial project where the class diagram is:

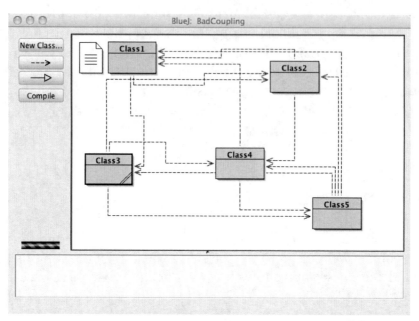

We say that a program like this has *high coupling*, which is something that should be avoided because of the maintenance nightmares that it will produce. For example, if I were to make a change to Class3 then I have to worry about how that change might affect all of the other classes because of the relationships between them that are shown by the arrows. So in general low coupling is good, high coupling is bad.

7.6 Exercises

General questions

1. When will an instance field usually get its initial value?

2. When will a class field usually get its initial value?

3. Explain the difference between a class field and an instance field.

4. What is another name for an instance field?

5. What are three other names for class fields?

6. A program intantiates three objects of a class. How many copies of any instance field will exist? How many copies of any class field will exist?

7. Where in the class definition will a class field usually be initialized?

8. Where in the class definition will an instance field usually be initialized?

9. Why do we need class fields in some programs? That is, why can't we just make them all instance fields?

10. Is high coupling good or bad? Why?

11. Why did I need to create the Stats class? That is, what advantages did I gain from having it?

In-lab programs

1. Extend the Player field so that it uses two class fields of type Stats to keep track of the total number of hits and at bats for all of the players that are instances of the field.

Out-lab programs

1. Extend the Student class from out-lab 1 in Chapter 2. Additional methods should include numStudents(), which returns the current number of student objects, and avgGPA(), which returns the gpa computed by taking the total number of grade points earned divided by the total number of credits taken. There should also be a new method getInfo(), which returns an object that contains the student's name, gpa, and number of credits completed. To do this, add a second class called StudentInfo whose instance fields contain these values.

2. Extend your Batsman class from the out-lab in Chapter 6 so that it uses class (static) fields to keep track of how many instances of Batsman have been created, the total number of runs scored by all of the batsmen, and the total number of times that they have been out. Create a method called numBatsmen() that returns the number of batsmen that have been created, and another called teamAverage() that computes the overall batting average for all of your batsmen. Add tests to your JUnit class and output the number

of batsmen and team average in your `main()` method.

3. Further extend the `Batsman` class to print out the names of the `Batsman` with the highest average and the bowler with the lowest average.

4. Further extend the Batsman class by adding a method `public void newInnings(int newRuns, int newBallsFaced, boolean out)` which updates a player's statistics after they have played a new innings. The parameter `out` will be `true` if the batsman was out, `false` if not out. All of the batsman's statistics should be updated. To update the batsman's high score, if needed, you'll need to use the code

```
if (newRuns > highScore)
    highScore = newRuns;
```

whose meaning should be obvious.

Chapter 8. Using Java's Online Documentation

8.1 Introduction

One of the great strengths of Java is that it has superb online documentation, which uses a system called Javadoc, and you should become comfortable using it as soon as possible. In this chapter I'll first give an example to show one way in which it can be very useful, and will then get into the online documentation in more detail. Then I will show how to use the Javadoc tool to generate equivalent documentation for your programs.

8.2 Why the Java Documentation Is Useful

It would be nice to be able to have a simple program like:

```
/*
 * Example for text
 * This one won't work - compile error
 * Author: Denbigh Starkey
 */

public class TestIt
{
    public static void main()
    {
        PrintStream terminal = System.out;
        terminal.println("Hello World!");
    }
}
```

with the reason that everything in Java has a class type, and that includes the object `out` in the class `System`, which has type class `PrintStream`. So you can assign the `System.out` value as the initial value of the variable `terminal`, which is also declared to be `PrintStream`, and then should just be able to say `terminal.println()` instead of `System.out.println()`. All this seems reasonable but if you try this, you'll get the compile error `cannot find symbol - class PrintStream`. Obviously something has gone wrong, so I'm going to use this to get into the Java API[28] documentation to not only find the problem but also to introduce a lot more information about Java's classes and something that I haven't discussed before, packages.

---

[28] **A**pplication **P**rogrammer (that's you now) **I**nterface.

8.3 Using the Online Documentation

Go to http://java.sun.com/javase/6/docs/api/, which is Sun's official documentation page for Java 6. You should get something like:

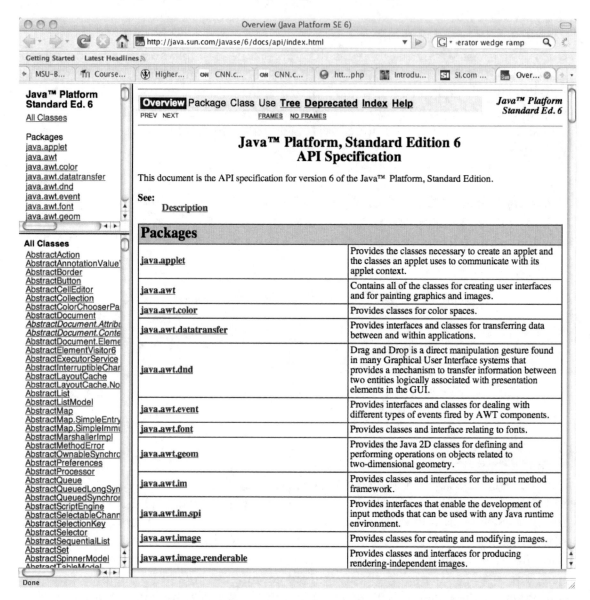

There are three panes here. The two thin panes on the left give access to all of the Java packages and classes.[29] The biggest pane shows more details on whatever you

---

[29] If you scan through the package and class lists you'll see that there are a lot of them.

are looking at, which initially is the package list. Note that packages begin with lowercase letters and classes with uppercase letters. I want to know why my program failed when I tried to use the declaration `PrintStream terminal = System.out;`, and my first suspicion is that `PrintStream` isn't really the type of `System.out`. Well we know that `out` is an object declared in class `System`, so scroll down through the class list until we get to `System` and click on that to see what it tells us. We'll get:

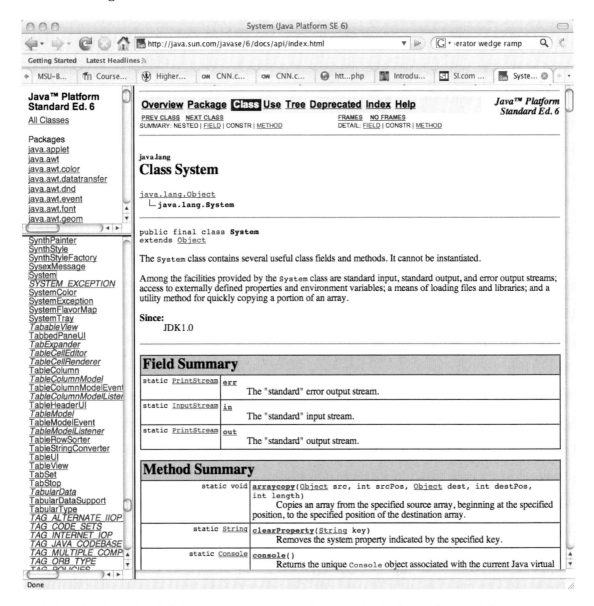

and if we look in the field summary, we see that `out` is declared here with type `PrintStream`, so that was correct for `System.out`. This still doesn't explain why the compiler couldn't find `PrintStream` because it obviously exists. So next I try clicking on the `PrintStream` link to see what that tells me and get:

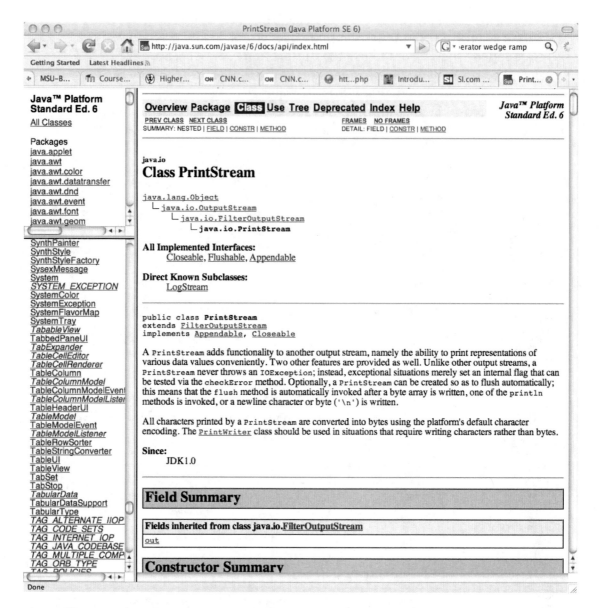

This tells us at the top that the class PrintStream is defined in the package java.io.printstream (we know that is a package not a class because it begins with a lowercase letter). Now we need an important piece of information, which is that when you run a Java program you are given access to everything in the System class, but not all of the packages, which are listed in the top left pane. To access information in any of them, you need to import the appropriate package using, in this case,

```
import java.io.PrintStream;
```

Now there are a lot of `java.io.something` (input/output) packages, so the usual approach is to use

```
import java.io.*
```

which will check your program and import any of the `java.io` packages that you need.[30] So if I change my program to:

```
import java.io.*;   // or java.io.PrintStream

public class TestIt
{
    public static void main()
    {
        PrintStream terminal = System.out;
        terminal.println("Hello World!");
    }
}
```

it will run correctly and output `Hello World!`.

The most common reason to use the online documentation is to see how Java's built-in classes and methods work (or sometimes to just search through a class' methods to see whether a method that you need has already been defined for you). For example, say that you want to learn more about the `replace` method that I used in the last chapter. If I try

```
String fruit = "banana",
       mess;
mess = fruit.replace("an", "x");
```

will it replace both occurrences of an to get `bxxa` or just the first to get `bxana`? The easiest way to find out is to go to the `String` class and scan through its methods to find out and you'll get:

---

[30] For those who have programmed in C/C++, this is similar to `#include <stdio.h>`

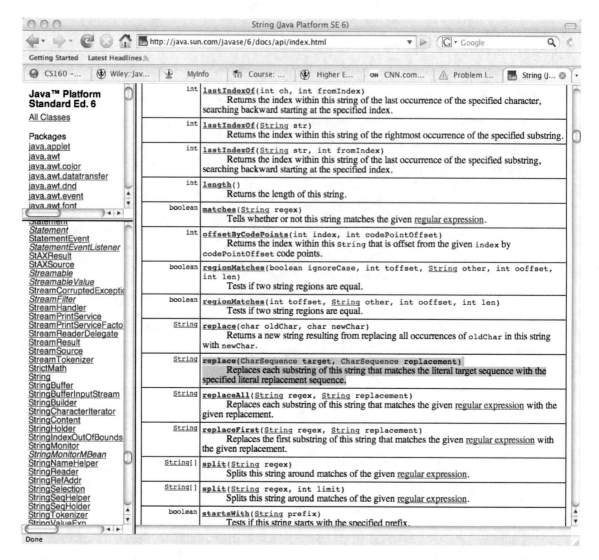

so the answer is that it will give you bxxa in this case. Note that if you wanted to just replace the first occurrence, there is another method, replaceFirst, which does this, but its format is a bit different because it uses a regular expression (regex), which I haven't introduced. However, it turns out that the simplest form of a regular expression is just a string and so one can just say

```
mess = fruit.replaceFirst("an", "x");
```

to get bxana. The summary also includes the return type for the methods, in this case both are String. If you need more information, then click on the replace link for examples and more detail.

8.4 Using Javadoc to Document Your Programs

In this chapter I've been encouraging you to use the Java 6 documentation to find out information about Java packages, classes, and their methods. All of this documentation was generated by Java's Javadoc system for producing documentation. This package is provided by Sun, the developer of Java. It can be downloaded and run if you aren't using a Java environment like BlueJ, but if you are using BlueJ, it is built in and trivial to use.

From now on I suggest that you get into the habit of using Javadoc every time that you write a program.

8.5 A Javadoc Example

I'll use the Player class that I developed in the last chapter. Even though it is a bad programming habit, I'll change the name instance field from `private` to `public`. This is only so that I can show what this will produce when I run Javadoc on the class.

To generate the Javadoc comments, all I have to do is to select Toggle Documentation View under the BlueJ menu (or use Ctrl-J or the Mac equivalent) and the display switches to the Javadoc view, automatically generated by BlueJ. For the Player class the first part of the developed documentation is shown on the screen shot on the next page.

There are some important things to notice about this documentation. The first is to notice how professional it looks, and all that I had to do to produce it was to do a single mouse click. Also notice that the form of the documentation is completely consistent with the online Java 6 documentation; this is because Javadoc was used to create that documentation from the Java system code. Finally, note that it follows the principles of encapsulation. That is, it only gives access to information that the user needs to know about. So the only instance or class field that is mentioned is name, because I changed it to public and left the others as private. If I had had any private methods, they would have been hidden.

If I had scrolled down through the documentation page, it would have showed me details on each of the public fields, constructors, and methods, but I haven't shown this image.

Java is the only language that I have used that has such superb documentation, both through the online documentation system and also through Javadoc's automatic documentation for user programs.

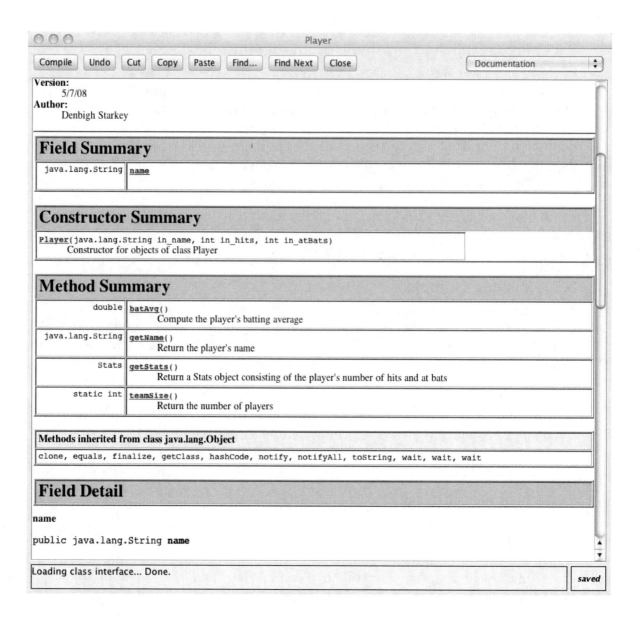

```
  ○ ○ ○                          Player
 [Compile] [Undo] [Cut] [Copy] [Paste] [Find...] [Find Next] [Close]        Documentation  ▲▼

 Version:
     5/7/08
 Author:
     Denbigh Starkey

 Field Summary
 java.lang.String  name

 Constructor Summary
 Player(java.lang.String in_name, int in_hits, int in_atBats)
         Constructor for objects of class Player

 Method Summary
          double  batAvg()
                    Compute the player's batting average
 java.lang.String  getName()
                    Return the player's name
           Stats  getStats()
                    Return a Stats object consisting of the player's number of hits and at bats
      static int  teamSize()
                    Return the number of players

 Methods inherited from class java.lang.Object
 clone, equals, finalize, getClass, hashCode, notify, notifyAll, toString, wait, wait, wait

 Field Detail
 name

 public java.lang.String name

 Loading class interface... Done.                                            saved
```

8.6 Exercises

General questions

1. As discussed earlier, the Javadocs for JUnit are at
    http://junit.org/junit/Javadoc/4.5/. Go to that page and select the
    Assert class. How many different method names are there in this class?

2. What do you think are the two most important classes in JUnit? Justify your
    answer.

3. Bring up the documentation for the Java Math class. How does one round a double value to the nearest long value? Repeat this question for double to int, float to long, and float to int.

4. Look at the field definitions in the documentation for the class Double. What is the largest possible double value that can be used, and what is the name of the constant with this value?

5. Still in the Double documentation, if I have a String value that can be interpreted as a double, how do I get that value? For example, how do I convert the string "3.14159" to the double value 3.14159? Will the same approach work for a long value? Where did you find the answer to the last part of this question?

6. Say that I want to compare two String values lexicographically (dictionary order) but I want to ignore whether the two strings use upper and/or lower case. One way would be to convert them both to upper case before comparing them, and another way would be to use a built-in method that ignores case when comparing them. Look through the String class to find the two methods that you need.

7. If in a program I need the value of the largest and smallest possible int values and the largest and smallest possible double values, what would I use? Look for them in the Integer and Double classes.

In-lab programs

1. Take the largest Java program that you have written so far, and fully document it with Javadoc comments. Look at the Javadocs documentaion that gets generated. From this point on you should do this for all of your programs.

Out-lab programs

1. There are no out-lab programs for this chapter because it didn't introduce any new programming concepts.

Chapter 9. Conditional Statements

9.1 Introduction

The modern way to teach OOP is called *objects first*, and this book follows this approach. The idea behind objects first is to get used to class definitions before getting into common programming structures. In this chapter and in chapter 11 I'll get into the two most important programming structures, conditional statements and loops. I've introduced a couple of examples of if statements, which are conditional statements, but now I can describe them more formally.

9.2 The Simple if Statement

The two most common forms of the if statement are the simple if-then and the if-then-else statements. The basic if-then or if statement has one of two forms:

```
if (condition)
    statement
```

and

```
if (condition)
    block of statements
```

A couple of technical things before I give examples:

(a) The condition is a boolean expression, which means anything that will evaluate to true or false. A typical example would be the expression x < 5, which would be true for values of x like -4 or 3, but false for values like 5 or 42. However, as we'll see later in this chapter, the expressions can be much more complex. For example, we might want to do something only if x > 7 and also y < 2. This leads to more complex expressions, which I'll get to later. For a while, though, just think that if it makes sense for an expression to have a value of either true or false, then this expression can be the condition in an if statement.

(b) The block of statements consists of any number of statements enclosed in braces, { and }.

I'll start by giving three examples of if statements:

```
if (courseSize <= 15)
    System.out.println("probably a senior or graduate course");
```

```
if (x < y)
{
    small = x;
    large = y;
}
```

```
double x = 7, y = 3;
if (x > y)
{
    double temp = x;
    x = y;
    y = temp;
}
System.out.println("x = " + x);
System.out.println("y = " + y);
```

In the first example the value of courseSize is compared to 15, and if it has a value that is less than or equal to 15, like 0, 11, or 15 (or any negative number), it will print out the prediction that this is probably a senior or graduate course.[31] If courseSize is greater than 15 (e.g., 75) it won't do anything.

In the second example either two statements will be executed or none. If x is less than y, then the variable named small is assigned the value of x and the variable named large is assigned the value of y. If the value of x is greater than or equal to the value of y, then nothing happens.

The third example is a bit more complicated, because it has a local variable, temp, inside the block. This code will sort x and y into ascending order. If x is less than or equal to y, it will do nothing, but if x is greater than y, the three assignments will exchange x and y's values. So whatever their incoming values are, at the end x will contain the smaller value and y the larger value. So in this case the output will be

```
x = 3
y = 7
```

Work through it to make sure that you agree that this is what happens.

Some programmers always use braces in conditional statements. For example, where I prefer to write:

```
if (x < y)
    small = x;
```

other programmers (maybe most others) prefer to write:

```
if (x < y)
{
    small = x;
}
```

---

[31] <= means "is less than or equal to."

This is a matter of programmer preference; choose one style and stick with it. Everyone agrees that the contained statement(s) should be indented to improve readability.

A source of programming problems can come from the fact that Java, like most other languages, has a null statement, which is a statement that only consists of the terminating semicolon, and that does nothing. The reason that this matters is that if, for example, you type the example that I had earlier as:

```
if (courseSize <= 15);
    System.out.println("probably a senior or graduate course";
```

then the prediction about this being a senior or graduate course will be output even if, say, courseSize is 75. The problem is the semicolon after the parentheses that hold the condition. Java will decide that this is ending a null statement, so in this case it will execute that null statement for small courses (which does nothing) and then always move on to the next statement, which is the println() statement. Remember that Java ignores indentations–they are just for the people reading the program. So *never* have an if statement that starts

```
if (condition);
```

with the trailing semicolon as it will always do nothing.

9.3 Arithmetic Comparison Operators

Before I get into more complex conditional statements, I'll describe Java's six arithmetic comparison operators, which let you compare numbers against each other:

Operator	Meaning
==	is equal to
!=	is not equal to
<	is less than
>=	is greater than or equal to
>	is greater than
<=	is less than or equal to

Note that these are three opposite pairs. So, for example, < and >= are opposites.

The meanings of these are obvious, but as one example, consider the following:

```
int x = 3,
    y = 7,
    z = 2;
if ((2 * x) != y)
    z = 5;
```

which will change the value of z to 2, but if y had been initialized to 6 instead of 7, it would have left the value of z unchanged at 2.

9.4 The if-then-else Statement

The simple `if` statement can be considered as a special case of the `if-then-else` which is also called the `if-else` statement.[32] This has the general form:

```
if (condition)
    statement or block of statements
else
    statement or block of ststements
```

The condition will be evaluated as usual, and if it evaluates to `true`, the first statement (or block of statements) will be evaluated. If, however, it evaluates to `false`, then the second statement (or block of statements) will be evaluated. So you can read it as "if this condition is true do these statement(s), otherwise do these statement(s)." For example:

```
if (x < y)
    small = x;
else
    small = y;
```

Here `small` will always get a value, the smallest of x and y (or the common value if x and y are equal). Or for a similar example with blocks of code

```
if (x < y)
{
    small = x;
    large = y;
} else {
    small = y;
    large = x;
}
```

---

[32] The word `then` is often included in the name of both this and the `if-then` statements because many predecessors of Java included the required keyword `then`. For example, in Algol, which is the major ancestor of languages like Java, one would have the statement:
```
IF (X < Y) THEN SMALL = X
              ELSE SMALL = Y
```

96

Now both `small` and `large` will always be assigned new values; if x is less than y, then `small` is set to x and `large` to y, but if x is greater than equal to y, then `small` gets y and `large` gets x.

Now let's take a more complicated example. Given three int values x, y, and z, I want save the smallest in small, middle value in middle, and largest in large. E.g., if x, y, and z are -5, 6, and 3, respectively, then I want to assign -5 to x, 3 to middle, and 6 to large. There are a number of ways I could do this. One, shown below, uses a nested if-then-else statement.

```
if (x < y)
{
    small = x;
    large = y;
}
else
{
    small = y;
    large = x;
}                        // small is smaller of x and y, large the larger

if (z < small)          // z is smaller than both
{
    middle = small;
    small = z;
}
else
{
    if (z < large)      // z is between the other two
        middle = z;
    else                // z is the biggest
    {
        middle = large;
        large = z;
    }
}
```

This is intended to show that conditional statements can be nested deeply inside each other. Trace through the logic to see how it works. I've added comments to make it a bit less complicated. Because the last, nested, if-then-else is considered a single conditional statement that contains inner statements, the braces ({ and }) around it are not needed, but are allowed.

9.5 A Common Mistake with boolean Valued Expressions

If an expression returns a `boolean` value, it is fairly common to get somewhat carried away with unnecessary `if-then-else` statements. For example, one often sees code like:

```
boolean xIsPos;
if (x > 0)
    xIsPos = true;
else
    xIsPos = false;
```

97

which looks reasonable at first glance, but if you look at what is happening, it says if the condition is `true`, return `true`, and if it is `false`, return `false`. It is much better to skip the `if-then-else` and just return the value of the condition as in:

```
boolean xIsPos = (x > 0);
```

9.6 Multiple Options: else-if Structures

The `if-then-else` statement essentially tells one what to do under two different options. Often things get more complicated than this. Say that a course is graded out of 100 and the instructor wants to give an A grade if a student's score is at least 90, a B if it isn't an A but is at least 80, a C if it isn't an A or B but is at least 70, a D if it isn't an A, B, or C but is at least 60, and an F otherwise. This is a natural for the else-if structure. In this case it would be:

```
if (score >= 90)
    grade = "A";
else if (score >= 80)
    grade = "B";
else if (score >= 70)
    grade = "C";
else if (score >= 60)
    grade = "D";
else
    grade = "F - sorry";
```

This is a very readable way to look at multiple options, and should be formatted in a consistent form like this.

The statement can contain as many `else-if` clauses as you want, and finishes with an optional `else` clause. If there is a final `else` clause exactly one of the statements or blocks of statements will be executed.

As another example, look again at the program segment that I gave in the last section that allocated three values to small. middle, and large. The nested conditional statement could be written better as:

```
if (x < y)
{
    small = x;
    large = y;
}
else
{
    small = y;
    large = x;
}                         // small is smaller of x and y, large the larger
// continued on next page
```

```
if (z < small)          // z is smaller than both
{
    middle = small;
    small = z;
}
else if (z < large)     // z is between the other two
    middle = z;
else                    // z is the biggest
{
    middle = large;
    large = z;
}
```

9.7 Multiple Options: The Switch Statement

The `else-if` structure worked well in the case where we had ranges of possible values, or in other similar situations. The `switch` statement is similar, but it is used when the options are specific values. For example, say that we are selling shoes and that the price of the shoes increases as the size increases, because bigger shoes need more leather. One way to do this would be to use an `else-if` structure like:

```
if (size == 6)
    price = "$44.99";
else if (size == 7)
    price = "$49.99";
else if (size == 8)
    price = "$54.99";
else if (size == 9)
    price = "$59.99";
else if (size == 10)
    price = "$64.99";
else if (size == 11)
    price = "$69.99";
else
    System.out.println("We don't sell this size");
```

but using a `switch` is preferred because it is easier to read. For this example the `switch` would be:

```
switch (size)
{
    case 6: price = "$44.99"; break;
    case 7: price = "$49.99"; break;
    case 8: price = "$54.99"; break;
    case 9: price = "$59.99"; break;
    case 10: price = "$64.99"; break;
    case 11: price = "$69.99"; break;
    default: Sytem.out.println("We don't sell this size"); break;
}
```

It begins with the keyword `switch`, followed by an expression in parentheses. Then the list of values in the `case` lines are compared against the expression's value, and if one matches, its statements are executed. If none match, then the `default` statements are executed.

A little complication is that it would be nice if Java were to leave the `switch` statement after executing the statements after a matching `case` value. Unfortunately it doesn't do this but it moves on and compares against the next `case` value. To stop it doing this, we use the `break` statement, which exits the `switch`. So *always* put the `break` statement, as shown, at the end of every `case` option line.

9.8 Comparing Floating Point Numbers for Equality

One important rule is to never directly use ==, !=, <= or >= to compare the values of two floating point variables, numbers, or expressions, but only use them to compare integer values. The problem with floating point numbers is that very small roundoff errors can make it appear that two floating point values are different. If you want to know whether two floating point values are equal, it is much safer to just check to see whether they are very close to each other, which means that the absolute value of their difference is less than some very small value that you define, typically called delta or epsilon. For example, it is considered very poor programming to say:

```
double x = 1.0 / 3.0;
if ((3.0 * x) == 3)
    System.out.println("3.0 * x is equal to 1.0");
```

because x, in decimal, could be something like 0.333333333333, so the danger is that $3.0 * x$ will be the binary equivalent of 0.999999999999, which is probably not equal to 1.0. Sometimes you'll get lucky and something like this will work; much of the time it won't. The correct way to do this is to use abs(), which is the absolute value method in the `Math` class, and say:

```
double x = 1.0 / 3.0,
       epsilon = 1.0E-9;

if (Math.abs((3.0 * x) - 1.0) < epsilon)
    System.out.println("3.0 * x is equal to 1.0");
```

The value that you choose for `epsilon` will depend on the application, but in most cases a value like 0.000000001 (which is $1.0E-9$) will work well, and I tend to use that unless I have a reason to use something different. This is similar to using tolerance values in assertEquals() calls in JUnit test classes.

So generalizing this, if, say, you want to test whether two floating point (i.e., `double` or `float`) values x and y are equal, use the test (`Math.abs(x - y) < epsilon`) for some small value of epsilon instead of the more obvious (`x == y`) test, which will fail sometimes because of roundoff errors. The same rule applies if only one of the values is floating point. For example, say we want to test whether 3 * x is equal to y after some code like:

```
double x;
int y;
// calculations that give x and y values
```

then we must use the test

```
if (Math.abs(3 * x - y) < epsilon) …
```

Any kind of equality check runs into potential roundoff problems. For example, say that x is a double and we want to check whether x is less than or equal to 7.4. Due to roundoff problems, an x value of 7.4 might have been calculated as, say, 7.40000000000001, and so a test like (x <= 7.4) will fail when it should succeed. To get around this, you should always accept any value less than 7.4 + epsilon, for some very small epsilon. That is, in this case we just need to use the test (x < 7.4 + epsilon). Similarly, if we want to test whether x is greater than or equal to 7.4, you should use (x > 7.4 - epsilon).

9.9 Comparing Strings for Equality and Alphabetic Order

Although the == operator is defined for string values, the results are very unpredictable. So, for example, if I try

```
String dept1 = "CS",
       dept2 = "cs".toUpperCase();  // converts cs to upper case

if (dept1 == "CS")
    System.out.println(dept1 + " (dept1) is CS");
else
    System.out.println(dept1 + " (dept1) is not CS");


if (dept2 == "CS")
    System.out.println(dept2 + " (dept2) is CS");
else
    System.out.println(dept2 + " (dept2) is not CS");
```

then the output will be:

```
CS (dept1) is CS
CS (dept2) is not CS
```

So in the first case Java recognizes that CS is equal to CS, but in the second case it doesn't. So the == is not guaranteed to work as expected when comparing string values. As a result, never use == between string values, but instead use the equals() method that is part of the built in string class. It is easiest to show this by example. The correct way to write the code, above, is:

101

```
String dept1 = "CS",
       dept2 = "cs".toUpperCase();  // converts cs to upper case

if (dept1.equals("CS"))
    System.out.println(dept1 + " (dept1) is CS");

if (dept2.equals("CS"))
    System.out.println(dept2 + " (dept2) is CS");
```

which will give the expected output:

```
CS (dept1) is CS
CS (dept2) is CS
```

So in summary, if you want to know whether two strings, `str1` and `str2`, are equal, never use (`str1 == str2`), but instead always use either (`str1.equals(str2)`) or `str2.equals(str1)`).

The values are either strings or string variables. For example,

```
if (first.equals("Denbigh"))
```

is the same as

```
if ("Denbigh".equals(first))
```

See the documentation for the `String` class in the online Java documentation for other types of comparisons that can be made on `String` values. One important method there is `compareTo()`, which compares two strings lexicographically (in dictionary order) and returns –1 if the first precedes the second, 0 if they are equal, and +1 if it follows the second. So, for example, "elk".`compareTo`("moose") is –1 but "moose".`compareTo`("elk") is +1, not the boolean `true` and `false` values that you might expect.

9.10 Constants (final Declarations)

This is a good time to detour briefly into how to effectively handle constants like the epsilon value. In the section on comparing floating point values I used the declaration and initialization

```
double epsilon = 1.0e-9;
```

when making comparisons between floating point values that include equality. So, for example, if x and y are floating point variables, then instead of the `boolean` comparison (x == y), you should use (`Math.abs`(x − y) < epsilon) and instead of (x <= y), you should use (x < (y + epsilon)). Once you've created epsilon you don't want it to be changed during execution, so in most languages

102

epsilon would be declared as a constant. In Java this is accomplished with the final keyword. E.g., the declarations

```
final double epsilon = 0.000001,
              piby2 = 1.570796;
```

will assign the values shown and will make them constants, not variables. If I were now to try a statement like:

```
piby2 = 1.5;
```

I'd get an error message like:

```
cannot assign a value to final variable piby2
```

Usually a final constant will be defined as shown here, where the declaration and the assignment are made at the same time, but this isn't always the case. The definition of a final constant just says that, once it is assigned, it cannot be changed, so one can declare it without an initial value and then later compute the value that one wants, assign that to the constant, and then have it protected against future modifications.

The final declarations in a class can be instance fields or class fields (declared as static). If they are declared as a class field, then they are usually declarations like the ones for epsilon and piby2, above, and it makes no sense for them to be copied into each instance of the class. If they are instance fields, then they are fixed value properties of each instance of the class. For example, if one has a class called BaseballTeam then one of the pieces of information one might maintain for each team could be when they first played. For example, for the Cubs this would be 1871 and for the Mariners 1977. Any time a new BaseballTeam object is added, this will be an instance field, but since it cannot change, it should be declared as final.

In Chapter 12, I'll introduce arrays, which are fixed size lists of values. Another use for final instance fields is with classes that contain an array as another instance field. If the size of the array is specified in the constructor, and the array is then created, then the size will be a final instance field. For example, the class definition might be something like:

```
public class ArrayClass
{
    // instance fields
    private final int size;
    private int[] intarray;  // declares an array but doesn't fix size

    /**
     * Constructor for objects of class ArrayClass
     */
    public ArrayClass(int in_size)
    {
        size = in_size;  // since it is final it can't be changed again
        intarray = new int[size]; // creates the array
        // assign values to the array
    }

    // public and private methods for the class omitted
}
```

Don't worry about the details yet, but with this code I've set up an array whose number of elements is size for each instance, where size is provided by a constructor parameter. Once the array is created, I don't want its size to be changed, and so size is set as a constant instance field, which could be different for each instance.

So in summary, constant declarations use the final keyword, and in most cases the initialization will be made at declaration time. Once a value has been assigned to a final constant, it cannot be changed later in the execution of the code.

9.11 The Selection Operator (Don't Use)

Java, following the example of C, has a selection operator, which essentially lets one put a condition on the right-hand side of an assignment statement. However, I recommend that you don't use it, at least until you get very confident with Java, and even then it is unkind to other people who read your programs. I'm introducing it here only so that you know what is going on if you see one in someone else's code.

Say one has the code:

```
if ((x % 2) == 0)
    y = x / 2;
else
    y = (x + 1) / 2;
```

that is very readable. If x is even (the remainder when divided by two is zero), y gets the value of x / 2, but if x is odd, y gets the value of (x + 1) / 2. The selection operator version of this is:

```
y = (x % 2) == 0 ? x / 2 : (x + 1) / 2;
```

104

which does the same thing, but isn't very readable unless you are used to looking at these things. So I recommend avoiding it, and I won't use it all in this book.

9.12 boolean (Logical) Operators

Say at the end of the semester an instructor wanted to send an annoying message saying You almost passed to any student whose final int score value was at least 50 but was below the passing 60 in that course. One way would be to use:

```
if (score >= 50)
    if (score < 60)
        System.out.println("You almost passed");
```

but this is ugly. Instead of this we can say:

```
if (score >= 50 && score < 60)
    System.out.println("You almost passed");
```

This is using the and operator, &&, and can be read as "if score is at least 50 and score is less than 60 then print out the annoying message."

Note that the following is not legal:

```
If (50 <= score < 60)  // not legal
    System.out.println("You almost passed");
```

Because 50 <= score returns true or false, so in effect you'd be trying to say true < 60 or false < 60, both of which make no sense.

Java has three boolean operators, && for and, || for or, and ! for not.

x && y: If x and y are boolean expressions, which means that they evaluate to true or false, then x && y is true if both x and y are true, and is false otherwise. This can be shown in a *truth table*:

&&	y is true	y is false
x is true	true	false
x is false	false	false

x || y: If x and y are boolean expressions, which means that they evaluate to true or false, then x || y is true if either x or y is true (this includes both being true), and is false otherwise. So x || y is only false if both x and y are false. This can also be shown in a truth table:

105

||	y is `true`	y is `false`
x is `true`	`true`	`true`
x is `false`	`true`	`false`

`!x`: If x is a `boolean` expression, which means that it evaluates to `true` or `false`, then `!x` is the opposite. So if x is `true`, then `!x` is false, and if x is `false`, then `!x` is true. For example, `(a > 7)` and `!(a <= 7)` are equivalent conditions.

9.12.1 Precedence of `boolean` Operators

An immediate question should be how we'll resolve ambiguities, which is the same problem that we had when introducing arithmetic operators. There the highest precedence went to the unary operators, followed by `*`, `/`, and `%`, with binary + and – lowest. Similar rules apply here. `!` has the highest precedence, followed by `&&`, with `||` lowest. For example, the expression:

```
!(x < y) && (y < z) || !(a == b) && (d != e)
```

is equivalent to the fully parenthesized:

```
(((!(x < y)) && (y < z)) || ((!(a == b)) && (d != e)))
```

In general, parentheses and spacing should be used to improve readability if logical expressions become complicated.

9.12.2 Short circuit evaluation of boolean expressions

In Java, and in most other modern languages, `&&` and `||` are evaluated using *short circuit* or *lazy* evaluation, which means that as soon as it knows the value of a boolean expression (`true` or `false`), it will stop evaluating any more components and will return that value. This sounds weird, and is most easily shown with an example. Say we have the expression:

```
int x, y, z;
// some code that gives them values

if ((x != 0) && (z == y / x))
    do something
```

consider what happens if x contains 0. The first part, `(x != 0)` will return `false`, and so at this point it is certain that the `&&` will return `false`, so Java will stop immediately without checking whether `z == y / x`. In this case it avoids a divide by zero that would have crashed the program. So under short circuit, if we are evaluating `x && y` and find that `x` is `false`, then we never evaluate `y` but just return that the `&&` is `false`.

A similar situation happens for `||` (the or operator). If we have `x || y` and find that `x` is `true`, then Java returns `true` for the `||` expression without ever evaluating `y`. For example, in

```
if ((x == 0) || (z == y / x))
    do something
```

`z == y / x` will only be evaluated if `x` is not zero.

9.13 Exercises

General questions

1. Write an `if` statement that outputs `You have a perfect grade` if the value of the `double` variable `score` is equal to `100.0`. Remember to be careful when comparing floating point values.

2. Write an `if` statement that outputs `You have passed the course` if the value of the `double` variable `score` is at least `60.0`.

3. Write an `if-then-else` statement that outputs `You have passed the course` if the value of the `double` variable `score` is at least 60.0, and outputs `You must take this course again` if its value is less than `60.0`.

4. Write an `if-then-else` statement that outputs `This is a valid grade` if the value of the `double` variable `score` is between `0.0` and `100.0`, and outputs `This is not a valid grade` otherwise.

5. Write code that increases the value of the `double` variable `score` by 10%. However, nobody can get more than 100, so if the increase takes the score higher than 100,reset the score to 100.0.

6. Why is the following code segment poor programming?

    ```
    double score;
    // other code that gives score a value
    if (score >= 50)
        // do something
    ```

    How would you improve the code?

107

7. Repeat Question 6, above, but with the condition (`score == 50`).

8. Why is a contitional statement that begins `if (name == "Susan")` poor programming. How would you fix it?

9. What will be output by the following code segment?

```java
int x = 5;
if (x < 3)
    System.out.println("A");
else if (x <= 10)
    System.out.println("B");
else if (x == 5)
    System.out.println("C"):
else
    System.out.println("D");
```

10. Give all reasons why an if the following code will not do what the programmer probably intended:

```java
if (x = 7);
    System.out.println(x);
```

Fix the code so that it does what was probably intended.

11. When will a switch statement be less effective than using an if-else-if statement?

12. When will an if-else-if statement be less effective than using a switch statement?

13. To make sure that you can read it, if you see one, give another example of the selection operator along with the equivalent code that doesn't use the operator.

In-lab programs

1. Modify the `Player` class from Chapter 2 so that it includes a method `reassign()` which outputs that a player should be reassigned to the minors if their batting average is below 2.20, outputs a message that the player should be considered for reassignment if their average is at least 2.20 but less than 2.60, and outputs a message that they should be retained if their average is at least 2.60. For example, a typical output might be: `Denbigh Starkey's batting average is 2.35, he should be considered for reassignment.`

2. Modify your class from in-lab 1, above, so that it outputs error messages if invalid parameters are entered. A player shouldn't have more hits that at bats, and neither should be negative. Also, if you attempt to compute a batting average when the number of at bats is zero, you should output an error message and avoid the exception.

Out-lab programs

1. Implement a Student class that has three instance fields, String name, the student's name, String major, which is one of CS, EE, and MATH, and double gpa. There will also be three class fields, all int, numCSMajors, numEEMajors, and NumMathMajors, with the obvious meanings. The only constructor gives values to the instance fields. In the constructor check to make sure that the gpa value is valid (between 0.0 and 4.0) and that the major is also valid. If not, output an error message. There will be four methods; getCSNumber(), getEENumber(), and getMathNumber(), with obvious meanings. There will also be a method averageGPA() which returns the average of the gpa values entered.

2. Modify the constructor in the Student class from 1, above, so that it accepts upper or lower case, or a mixture, for the major. E.g., CS could be entered as CS, Cs, cS, or cs. Use toUpperCase to do this.

3. Modify the methods so that they only use data from valid inputs. So if an object is created with an invalid major and/ot gpa, it will not be used in the cumulative values.

4. Ensure that the averageGPA doesn't divide by zero if no valid CS, EE, or Math students have been created.

Chapter 10. Taking Control of Input/Output

10.1 Introduction

Using `System.out.print` and `System.out.println` can be a pain at times, and also makes it hard to accomplish some very simple formatted output. For example, say one wants to print out the scores for three students, `score1`, `score2`, and `score3` with an aligned output like

```
Student1's current score is  80 points
Student2's current score is   5 points
Student3's current score is 100 points
```

then one could try three `println` method calls as in

```
System.out.println("Student1's current score is " + score1 + " points");
System.out.println("Student2's current score is " + score2 + " points");
System.out.println("Student3's current score is " + score3 + " points");
```

but this will give the output

```
Student1's current score is 80 points
Student2's current score is 5 points
Student3's current score is 100 points
```

without the alignment that I wanted.

Another problem is with floating point numbers where, for example, the statement `System.out.println(3.0 / 7.0);` will output `0.42857142857142855`, but in most cases I'd like to be able to control the precision and say, for example, that I want this to be rounded to three decimal places, in this case `0.429`.

The alternative is to use `System.out.format()`. The first example would become:

```
System.out.format("Student1's current score is %3d points%n", score1);
System.out.format("Student2's current score is %3d points%n", score2);
System.out.format("Student3's current score is %3d points%n", score3);
```

which will give me the formatted output that I showed above.

10.2 Structure of a format() Method Call

A call to `System.out.format` has the form:

```
System.out.format("control string", output expressions);
```

The control string consists of a string of characters that includes (if there is at least one output expression) some control codes. This system is copied almost exactly from C's `printf()` statement. The major codes are shown in the table below.

b, B	general	A boolean argument will be output as true or false if %b is used, TRUE or FALSE if %B is used.
h, H	general	The argument will be output as a hexadecimal number. For example, if x is 1005, then it will be output as 3ed if %h is used, 3ED if %H is used.
s, S	general	This will print out a string. For example, if x is "Denbigh" then it will be output as Denbigh if %s is used, DENBIGH if %S is used.
c, C	character	Outputs a character. If %C is used, a letter will be in uppercase.
d	integral	Prints out a decimal integer.
o	integral	Prints out an octal (base 8) integer.
x, X	integral	Prints out a hexadecimal (base 16) integer.
e, E	floating point	Prints out a decimal number in scientific notation. E.g., 123.456 would print as 1.23e+02 using %.2e, 1.23E+02 using %.2E.
'f'	floating point	The result is formatted as a decimal number.
g, G	floating point	The result is formatted using scientific notation or decimal format, depending on the precision and the value after rounding.
%	percent	The result is a literal '%'.
n	line separator	The result is the platform-specific line separator.

When used, these will all be preceded with a % to designate that they are codes. The two simplest are %%, which lets one print out a % without Java thinking that it is a code designator (this is called escaping the character), and %n, which terminates the current line.

Apart from %% and %n, the number of codes in the string should match the number of expressions in the output expressions list, and their types should match exactly.

Many codes have optional width codes (e.g., %4d will print out an integral value in a width of four characters) and in some cases an optional precision, which is preceded with a period (e.g., %5.3f has a width of five including three digits after the decimal point).

112

This all looks complex and messy, so will most easily be made clear with a few examples:

```
double x = 2.0 / 3.0;
char c = 'd';
int y = 777;
System.out.format("x = %4.2f%c%4d%n", x, c, y);
```

will output

```
x = 0.67d 777
```

Track through this and make sure that it makes sense. Note that x has been rounded to 0.67 when the code asked for two decimal places. Also note that, since this is the first time that I've used the char primitive type, it is designated with single quotes, as compared to the double quotes used for string values.

```
double x = -2.0 / 3.0;
char c = 'd';
int y = 777;
System.out.format("x = %5.3f%c%4d%n", x, c, y);
```

will output

```
x = -0.667d 777
```

The new feature here is that I've asked Java to print x with three decimal digits, in a width of four. This is impossible because -0.667 requires a width of six, so it has ignored me and treated this as though it were just %.3f.

```
String first = "Susan", last = "Starkey";
char middle = 'M';
int usnaGrad = 2002, wings = 2004;
System.out.format("%s %c. %S%n%nGraduated: %d, wings: %d%n",
                  first, middle, last, usnaGrad, wings);
```

will output:

```
Susan M. STARKEY

Graduated: 2002, wings: 2004
```

There are a number of things going on here.

- The %n%n in the middle of the string causes the spacing shown (two end of line characters).
- There are five codes (not counting the three %n codes) and also five arguments, so they match.
- When I used the code %s, the string Susan appeared as it was in the variable first, but when I used %S, Starkey was converted to STARKEY (the same thing happens with %c and %C for characters).

113

- I could have used %4d instead of %d, or even replaced `Graduated %d` with `Graduated%5d`, but there was no reason to do this.

```
int x = 13579;
System.out.format("x = Decimal: %d, Octal: %o, Hex: %X%n", x, x, x);
```

will output

```
x = Decimal: 13579, Octal: 32413, Hex: 350B
```

as `%o` and `%x` convert numbers to octal and hexadecimal before printing them.

10.2.1 Left and right justification of output values

If you print out a number with a field width that is greater that the number of characters needed by the value then it will be preceded by the number of spaces needed (i.e., it will be right justified in the field). However if you specify the field width as a negative number the value will be output left justified. For example:

```
System.out.format("%-15s %13s%n",  "First name:", "Susan");
System.out.format("%-15s %13s%n",  "Last name:", "Starkey");
System.out.format("%-15s %13s%n",  "Complete name:", "Susan Starkey");
```

will output:

```
First name:        Susan
Last name:        Starkey
Complete name: Susan Starkey
```

The most common use of this is with strings, but it also works with numbers. For example, if you output -3.45 with a format code of %-6.1f Java will output -3.5 followed by two spaces.

10.3 System.out.printf()

`System.out.printf()` is an alias for `System.out.format()`, and so if you prefer, you can use that method name in all of the examples without any change in the results. The method name `printf()` was added to provide comfort for old C programmers because that was C's name for their formatted output. I recommend that you use the more reasonable `format()` name. As I will show below, this is required when using `String.format()` since `String.printf()` doesn't exist.

10.4 Other Uses for format()

One usually thinks of the format() method as a way to output information, but it can also be used to create strings from multiple information sources. As an example, say one has Susan's first and last names and her middle initial, and wants to build a string with her full name, then the following code will do this:

```
String first = "Susan",
        last = "Starkey";
char mi = 'M';
String name = String.format("%s %c. %s", first, mi, last);
System.out.println(name);
```

and the println() method will output Susan M. Starkey. Note that this use of format() is from the String class. In the String class printf() has not been included as an alias for format(), and so String.printf() will not be recognized.[33]

You'll find that there are many times when you want to do this sort of thing, and using format() is usually much cleaner than other approaches.

10.5 Reading Values from the Input Stream

Most of you have already read in inputs in lab using a scanner, but this chapter will go into this a bit deeper and will also introduce I/O through pop-up dialog boxes.

Input in Java isn't very clean, but it is better than it was in the earlier versions of the language. One would hope that since output is handled by using

```
System.out.println(n);
```

Then maybe input would be handled by something like

```
n = System.in.getInt();
```

but unfortunately this doesn't exist. Instead one needs to instance a Scanner object, as I'll show in the next section.

10.6 Instancing and Using a Scanner Object

Whenever one wants to read an input value into a Java program, there are two steps; first one must instance an object of class Scanner, which is usually called in,

---

[33] Look in the method summary for the String class in the Java 6 documentation, and you'll find format, but you won't find printf in the list.

and then one uses methods with names like `nextInt()` and `nextDouble()` to input values. `Scanner` is in the package `java.util.Scanner`, and so if, for example, one wants to first input an int n and then input a double d from the input stream, the code will be:

```
import java.util.*; // gets me java.util.scanner
...
Scanner in = new Scanner(System.in);
...
System.out.println("Enter an integer value for n");
n = in.nextInt();
System.out.println("Enter a double value for d");
d = in.nextDouble();
```

The `import` statement is needed to get the `Scanner` class.

`Scanner in = new Scanner(System.in);` instances `in` as a scanner. Unless you are using other ways like dialog boxes or file input to get input from Java, you'll probably have this line in every significant Java program that you write.

Both `n = in.nextInt();` and `d = in.nextDouble()` read in values typed by the user and assign them to n and d, respectively. Note that they are both preceded by `println` statements that tell the user to enter a value. This is critical. An output statement that tells the user that they should enter a value should precede every input statement, because otherwise they would never know when to do that. This is called *prompting* for an input.

As you probably expect, `Scanner` also has methods `nextByte()`, `nextShort()`, `nextLong()`, `nextFloat()`, and `nextBoolean()`.

When retrieving input values they can be on individual lines or on the same line. For example, if `in` is a `Scanner` instance defined as above and we have

```
System.out.println("Enter values for n, d, and b");
n = in.nextInt();
d = in.nextDouble();
b = in.nextByte();
```

then one could satisfy this with one line containing, say,

```
5       2.7 3
```

or three lines containing

```
5
2.7
3
```

or a mixture like

116

```
     5

2.7 3
```

Technically input values are separated by *whitespace*, although this can be changed to much more complicated separation systems.

10.7 String Input

If you look at the methods that can be applied to the object `in` from the `Scanner` class in the Java 6 documentation, you'll see that there aren't methods called `nextString()` or `nextChar()`. The reason for this is because there is no way to decide where the next string is. For example, say one had

```
n = in.nextInt();
s = in.nextString();
d = in.nextDouble();
```

and the input line

```
3    ab    4.2
```

what is the string? Is it just "ab", or is it ab with some surrounding spaces like " ab " or "ab "?

To handle this problem there are two solutions; one uses the `nextLine()` method, which returns the next line of input as a `String`, and the other uses `next()`, which in this case would return the string ab. I'll look at `nextLine()` first and then `next()`.

10.7.1 nextline()

Say that s, n, and d have types `String`, `int`, and `double`, respectively, and one has:

```
s = in.nextLine();
n = in.nextInt();
d = in.nextDouble();
System.out.println(s);
System.out.println(n);
System.out.println(d);
```

and the input is

```
Denbigh Starkey
4 33.2
```

then the output will be

```
Denbigh Starkey
4
33.2
```

A thing to be careful of is that even though it sounds as though `nextLine()` always grabs the next line, if the current line hasn't been terminated, it actually returns the rest of the current line. For example, say one has, with the same types as I had in the last example, the code segment

```
n = in.nextInt();
s = in.nextLine();
d = in.nextDouble();
System.out.println(n);
System.out.println(s);
System.out.println(d);
```

you might be surprised when Java blows up when given the input

```
3
Denbigh Starkey
4.5
```

with a `InputMismatchException` message. What has happened is that Java finds the 3 on the first line and assigns it to n, as expected. However, it is still on the first line and so it now assigns the rest of that line, which is the null or empty string, to s. Then, when it looks for the `double` named d, the next thing that it finds is the token `Denbigh`, which can't be interpreted as a `double`, so it dies with the exception described. So if one is mixing `nextInt()` or other methods with `nextLine()`, make sure that lines are terminated first. One way to do this without getting into some of the trickier features is to use `nextLine()` to clear things out. For example, in the example above I could have used:

```
n = in.nextInt();
s = in.nextLine();
s = in.nextLine();
d = in.nextDouble();
```

After finding the value 3 and assigning it to n, the first `nextLine()` would have cleared out the rest of the first line, with the second `nextLine()` the string s would have been given the value `Denbigh Starkey`, and with `nextDouble()` d gets the value 4.5.

10.7.2 next()

This grabs the next *token* (which is a chunk of non-whitespace characters) from the input and returns it as a string. So getting back to an earlier example, if the input is:

```
3    ab    4.2
```

and we use

```
n = in.nextInt();
s = in.next();
d = in.nextDouble();
```

then n will get 3, s will get ab, and d will get 4.2, as we probably hoped.

10.8 Dialog Boxes For Input

A completely different way to do I/O is through a *dialog box*, which is a pop-up box that lets the user input or output values. These are most commonly used for input, and so I'll look at input dialog boxes first.

Dialog boxes are defined in the class JOptionPane, which are part of the Swing packages, so any program that uses dialog boxes must use

```
import javax.swing.*;
```

Using a dialog box is most easily described with an example. If we have the code segment:

```
String inString;
JOptionPane myin = new JOptionPane();
inString = myin.showInputDialog("Enter instructor's name");
System.exit(0);  // always include, it is described below
```

BlueJ will first display the popup dialog box:

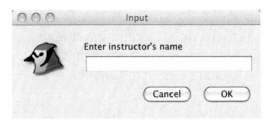

and then if I enter my name:

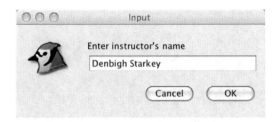

and click OK `Denbigh Starkey` will be assigned to `inString`.

I didn't really need to declare the variable `myin`, but I find it convenient, in particular if I have a number of inputs that I will be making through dialog boxes. However, the following code segment will do exactly the same as the previous one:

```
String inString;
inString = JOptionPane.showInputDialog("Enter instructor's name");
System.exit(0);
```

Whenever you use dialog boxes (input or output), put the statement `System.exit(0)` at the end of your main program. This kills off an extra thread that is created for the user interface, which will be left hanging if you don't do this.

If you are using a dialog box to enter a value that is, say, numeric, then you'll need to convert the `String` value that the box gives you to the appropriate numeric type. There are, of course, methods to do this. `Double.parseDouble(stringval)` converts a string to a double, and `Integer.parseInt(stringval)` converts a string to an int. I'll give a short program, consisting of just a `main()` method, that demonstrates this after I've described using a dialog box for output.

10.9 Dialog Boxes for Output

This also uses the `JOptionPane` class, with the method `showMessageDialog` instead of the `showInputDialog` method that was used for an input dialog box. The usual form is

```
outbox.showMessageDialog(null, a String value to be output)
```

where `outbox` is an instance of `JOptionPane`. Don't worry about the `null` parameter, technically it is selecting a default parent frame, which will work in most cases, so until you get multiple frames always include `null` as the first parameter and don't worry why. For example, we might have:

```
outbox.showMessageDialog(null, "Radius: " + radius +
                               ", Area: " + area);
```

Or, if you want format control, you could output this with, say,

120

```
String outString = String.format("Radius: %.2f, Area: %.2f", radius,
                                  area);
```

10.10 Example Program for I/O Dialog Boxes

I'll give a program to read in the radius of a circle from a dialog box, compute the area, and output the radius and the area to an output dialog box. To do this it will have to read the value in as a string, convert that into a double, and then use `Math.PI * radius * radius` to compute the radius of the circle. Remember that the `Math` class provides the value of π as `Math.PI`. I'll just use a simple `main()` method.

```
import javax.swing.*;

public class DialogTest
{
    public static void main()
    {
        String inString;   // string value from dialog box
        double radius,     // radius converted from instring
               area;       // area of the circle
        JOptionPane inBox = new JOptionPane(),  // dialog box
                    outBox = new JOptionPane(); // dialog box
        inString = inBox.showInputDialog("Enter radius");
        radius = Double.parseDouble(inString);
        area = Math.PI * radius * radius;

        outBox.showMessageDialog(null, "Radius: " + radius +
                                 ", Area: " + area);

        System.exit(0);
    }
}
```

This program uses a dialog box to read in a value as a string, which is then converted into a double and saved in radius. If `2.1` is entered into the input dialog box, then there will be a popup output pane:

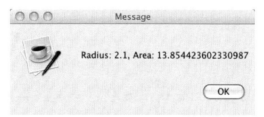

If instead of the + form for String composition I use the `String.format()` method as shown earlier, or in one statement with:

```
outbox.showMessageDialog(null,
    String.format("Radius: %.2f, area: %.2f", radius, area));
```

then the value in the output pane for area would become the more reasonable;

```
Radius: 2.10, area 13.85
```

I recommend always using `String.format()` in dialog box output because it gives you far greater control over your output quality.

10.11 Exercises

General questions

1. What, if any, is the difference between `System.out.format("%d%n", x);` and `System.out.printf("%d%n", x);`?

2. Assume that I have a `Scanner` object named `in` and that the next two lines of input contain `Denbigh` and `Denbigh Starkey`, respectively. If I try:

   ```
   first = in.next();
   fullName = in.nextLine();
   ```

   why won't `fullName` get the string "`Denbigh Starkey`"? How can you fix this?

3. If the value 123.45 is output with %5.2f and %-5.2f will there be any difference?

4. What, exactly, will be output by the following? Show each space as an underscore.

   ```
   double x = 123.4,
          y = -17.88;
   int    z = -37;
   String name = "Susan";
   System.out.format(" %7.2f%-7.2f%%%2d%n%n%-6s%4s",
                     x, y, z, name, name);
   ```

In-lab programs

1. Use JOption panes to read in five double values, one at a time, and output their average value and their largest and smallest values (a) using a JOptionPane and (b) to the standard output window. Give prompts for input and use String.format() to give good looking output.

2. Modify in-lab 1, above, so that it reads all five values from a single JOptionPane call.

3. Write a method `public static void calHeader(String monthName)` which outputs a header for a calendar. The seven days (Sunday, ...) should be output equally spaced with the name of the month centered above them. To output, say, n spaces, you can use the code

```
for (int i = 0; i < n; i++)
    System.out.format(" ");
```

which could be useful when centering the month name for different length months. Loops like this will be introduced in the next chapter.

Out-lab programs

1. Modify the first in-lab, above, so that it first outputs the input values to the standard output, on one line with the values separated by commas.

2. Read in six double values using a Scanner object and output them on two lines with three values per line. The values should be aligned and each value should be output with two decimal places and a field width that is one greater than the size of the widest value entered.

Chapter 11. Looping Statements

11.1 Introduction

Until now when we've done something, it has essentially been a single operation each time. The strength of a computer, however, is its ability to do things repeatedly. So, for example, at the end of the semester an instructor will want the computer to compute the weighted grades for all the students in their class, and wouldn't want to have to individually say that they want the computer to compute each student's grade since by the time that they made it to the names beginning with about D in a large class they'd be infuriated. In this chapter I'll be looking at Java's statements for doing related things again and again.

One concept that I won't have here is arrays. Arrays are a natural companion for looping statements, and so when we get to them in Chapter 12 we'll see additional uses for loops.

11.2 Example: Summing the First *n* Integers

I'll take a simple example and show how to program it with three different Java looping structures. Follow these initial examples carefully and try to get the basic idea about what is going on here, and then in the subsequent sections I'll describe these looping statements in detail. If you have previously programmed in C or C# you will find that these statements are very familiar.

The problem will be to find the sum of the first *n* integers, where *n* will be an input value.[34] So, for example, if the value of *n* is 10, then we want to compute $1 + 2 + ... + 10$, which is 55.

The examples will be similar. They will all start by initializing an integer variable called sum to 0, and then will add first 1 to sum to get 1, then add 2 to get 3, and so on until it finishes after it adds the value of *n*. We'll just see different ways to do this. For all three statements I'll also assume that I've declared the variables sum and n, have initialized sum to 0, and have read a value into n from the input stream. That is, I've executed some code like:

---

[34] I know that there is a better way to compute this, which is to just compute n * (n + 1) / 2, but the point of this example is to show the looping statements, not to show off the best solution to the problem.

```
int sum = 0,   // keep a running total of the sum of n integers
    n;          // input value which tells how many integers to sum
Scanner in = new Scanner(System.in);  // sets up input scanner

System.out.println("Enter the value for n");
n = in.nextInt();
```

I'll also assume that after the looping statement I'll be printing out the result with a statement like:

```
System.out.format("The sum of the first %d integers is %d%n", n, sum);
```

which will give me an output like

```
The sum of the first 10 integers is 55
```

11.2.1 Approach 1: The while loop

The while statement (also called the while loop) for this problem is:

```
// assert sum has been set to zero and a value for n has been
// input, as described above
int i = 1;
while (i <= n)
{
    sum += i;
    i++;
}
```

The while loop keeps executing the statements inside the braces as long as its condition (here the condition is (i <= n)) is true. Say n is 3. Initially i is 1, and 1 <= 3, so it adds 1 to sum, which was 0, to give sum the value 1, and then adds 1 to i to make it 2. We now redo the statement starting at the condition, which is 2 <= 3, so we add 2 to sum to make it 3 and add 1 to i to make it 3. Go back to the top of the while statement and check the condition 3 <= 3. We add 3 to sum to make it 6 and 1 to i to make it 4. Go back to the top and check the condition; 4 <= 3 fails, so we are done with the while statement and sum has the value 6 which is the value of 1 + 2 + 3.

Looking at this in a different way, track the values of n, sum, i, and the while condition, and also the statements executed as we enter the loop for n = 3, as shown in the table below.

	n	sum	i	i <= n	actions
1st time at loop	3	0	1	true	sum += i; i++;
2nd time at loop	3	1	2	true	sum += i; i++;
3rd time at loop	3	3	3	true	sum += i; i++;
4th time at loop	3	6	4	false	exit loop

Make sure that you follow this. A good test is to look at the code

```
// assert sum has been set to zero and a value for n has been
// input, as described above

int i = 0;
while (i < n)
{
    i++;
    sum += i;
}
```

and go through the same analysis for n = 3 to show that it also works.

11.2.2 Approach 2: The `for` statement

The `for` statement for this problem will be

```
// assert sum has been set to zero and a value for n has been
// input, as described above

for (int i = 1; i <= n; i++)
    sum += i;
```

which is a shorthand version of the first while loop, above. This loop only controls a single statement, sum += i;, and so it doesn't need braces. It has three parts in parentheses separated by semicolons. The first part declares a loop control variable named i and initializes it to 1; the second part gives the loop control condition; and the third part shows how i should be changed at the end of each loop. Note that these three match up exactly with the statements and condition in the first while loop in Section 11.2.1.

The `for` loop can be read as:

(a) set i to 1.
(b) only enter the loop each time if i <= n.
(c) At the end of each loop add one to i.

127

which is the same as the `while` statement.

11.2.3 Approach 3: The `do-while` Statement

The do-while statement for this problem will be:

```
// assert sum has been set to zero and a value for n has been
// input, as described above
int i = 1;
do
{
    sum += i;
    i++;
} while (i <= n);
```

This looks similar to the regular `while` statement, but instead of checking the condition at the beginning of the block, it is checked at the end of the block. A consequence of this is that whereas in a `while` loop it is possible that the statements in the block will not be executed at all (when the condition is false when we first enter the block), with a `do-while` the statements will always be executed at least once. So in this case, if we read in 0 for n, then the `while` loop will return 0 as the value of sum, but the `do-while` will return 1.

11.3 The `for` Statement

Now I'll look at all three of these loop statements in more detail, starting with the `for` statement because it is the most commonly used.

The `for` loop exists in some form in all major programming languages. The general form of the Java `for` statement is

```
for (initialize; loopCondition; modifier)
    statement or block of code
```

Initialize: This first part of the `for` statement will usually be used to set an initial value for a variable called the *loop control variable*, and in many cases to declare it. So typical statements here are int i = 1; or j = 0;.[35]

It is generally agreed that it is best to declare the loop control variables in each `for` statement, although this isn't always practical. So typically a `for` statement will begin:

```
for (type varname = initval; …)
```

---

[35] The most common names for loop control variables are i, j, and k, which goes back to naming conventions in the original Fortran in the 1950s.

and not just

```
for (varname = initval; …)
```

If you do use the second form, and declare the loop control variable earlier, then you can access the last value of the loop control variable outside the loop, but this is considered to be dangerous programming, and hence poor programming.

LoopCondition: The loop control condition will be tested each time that the loop is about to begin, including the first time that the `while` loop is entered. If it is `true`, the loop statement or block of statements is executed, and then we move back to the top of the loop again. If it is `false`, then that completes this loop and control passes to the statement after the loop.

Modifier: This will usually change the value of the loop control variable in some way, most commonly by adding a fixed amount to it each time. Decrements are also common where we subtract a fixed amount each time. The modifier is executed after executing the loop statement or block of statements and before the loop control condition check is made.

11.3.1 Another `for` example

I'll be giving a lot more examples of `for` loops when we get to arrays, but for now I'll look at one more example. I want a method to find the total of a number of doubles in the input stream. These values will be preceded by an integer that gives the number of doubles. So if the input contains, for example

```
6
-3.2 1.0 4.25 1.1
3.32 2.1
```

then we want to compute the value `8.57`, which is the total of the six doubles. The code, in a class with a `main` method, could be:

```
public static double sumins()
    {
        Scanner in = new Scanner(System.in);
        double sum = 0,  // running total of input values
               n;        // number of input values
        System.out.println("Enter # of doubles to be summed");
        n = in.nextInt();
        for (int i = 1; i <= n; i++)
            sum += in.nextInt();
        return sum;
    }
```

11.3.2 Things to avoid

The `for` statement is far more general than I have shown because, for example, all three of its components are optional (it is even possible to find uses for a `for` statement that has the form `for (;;)`, where all three components are empty), or can contain more complex structures. For example, the segment

```
int result = 0;
for (int i = 0, j = 6; i < 5; i++, j += 2)
    result += i + j;
```

would output 60, which is the sum $0 + 6 + 1 + 8 + 2 + 10 + 3 + 12 + 4 + 14$, which is what you should expect if you track through this complex loop. Both `i` and `j` are loop control variables and each time that the loop runs 1 is added to `i` and 2 to `j`. Execution continues as long as `i < 5`. However, while this is cute, it is considered a poor use of the `for` loop. A `for` loop should be restricted to a single control variable, and it should have a simple loop control condition and a simple and consistent increment.

11.4 The while Statement

The general form of the `while` statement is

```
while (condition)
    statement or block of statements
```

The condition is evaluated first, and if it is `true`, then the loop statement(s) are executed and then control goes back to the top of the loop where the condition is checked again. This continues until the condition is `false` at which point that finishes the loop and control is passed to the statement after this `while` loop. For example, the `for` loop in my last example could be written:

```
int i = 1;
while (i <= n)
{
    sum += in.nextInt();
    i++;
}
```

but clearly the `for` version is easier to read and so is preferred. As a result the `while` is usually restricted to cases where the `for` loop solution is ungainly. For example, say that one wants to read in and sum an unspecified number of positive doubles. We are going to need to tell the computer when we are done, and so one option is use an input of `-1.0` as a *sentinel value* at the end. This way we can keep reading in values and continue summing them as long as the value is positive. We can write this in a few ways, and a couple of options follow:

```
double sum = 0.0,    // running total of input values
       inval = 1.0; // latest input value. Initialized to zero
                    // so while condition is satisfied on entry
System.out.println("Enter positive values to be summed");
System.out.println("Use -1 as input to terminate");
while (inval > 0)
{
    inval = in.nextDouble();
    if (inval > 0)
        sum += inval;
}
```

In this version the `while` loop statements input a value into `inval` and only adds the value to `sum` if it is positive. The loop condition makes sure that the latest value of `inval` is positive, and if it isn't, it exits. To ensure that the condition is true, the first time that we execute the loop `inval` is initialized to a positive value.

```
boolean notdone = true;  // used to control while loop
double sum = 0.0, // running total of input values
       inval;      // latest input value

System.out.println("Enter positive values to be summed");
System.out.println("Use -1 as input to terminate");
while (notdone)
{
    inval = in.nextDouble();
    if (inval > 0)
        sum += inval;
    else
        notdone = false;
}
```

Here I've controlled the loop with a `boolean` named `notdone`, which is initialized to `true`. We keep reading in values and adding them to `sum` as long as they are positive; when we get a negative input value (or zero) `notdone` is changed to `false` and that will stop the `while` loop.

Some people prefer to name the `boolean` control variable `done`, in which case it will be initialized to `false` and will be changed to `true` when a negative value is input. The `while` loop header will become

```
while (!done)
```

11.5 The do-while Statement

As discussed earlier the `do-while` is similar to the `while`, with the difference in the `do-while` the condition is checked after the loop statements are executed, not before. As a result, some `while` loop code will be executed zero times, whereas with a `do-while` the code will always be executed at lease once. Take the example that I used for `while` where we sum positive doubles until a negative number is input. Using a `do-while` one solution is:

```
double sum = 0.0, // running total of input values
       inval;     // latest input value

System.out.println("Enter positive values to be summed");
System.out.println("Use -1 as input to terminate");
do
{
    inval = in.nextDouble();
    if (inval > 0)
        sum += inval;
} while (inval > 0);
```

Note that this is in some ways cleaner than the two while loop versions, since I haven't had to initialize inval to an artificial value or to use a boolean to control the loop. The loop is always executed, but in this case that doesn't cause any problems because if, for example, the first input value is -1, signifying that we don't have any positive input values to sum, the program segment will leave sum at 0.0, which is what we want.

Another do-while solution is:

```
double sum = 0.0,    // running total of input values
       inval = 0.0;  // latest input value, initialized to zero
                     // as required in the loop

System.out.println("Enter positive values to be summed");
System.out.println("Use -1 as input to terminate");
do
{
    sum += inval;  // inval must be initialized to zero
    inval = in.nextDouble();
} while (inval > 0);
System.out.println(sum);
```

which gets rid of the if statement in the loop code, but needs inval to be initialized to 0.0 since it is added to sum before any inputs are retrieved. Of the four while and do-while code segments shown this is the one that I would use for this problem.

11.6 The foreach Statement (Preview)

This is a relatively new statement in Java because it was first added in Java 5. It is based on the foreach statement that Perl programmers use extensively. Its primary use is with arrays, and so I'll wait until I've described arrays before I describe it.

11.7 The BlueJ Debugger

In Chapter 4, when discussin debugging programs, I mentioned that as programs become more complex the BlueJ debugger will often greatly simplify finding logical errors in your programs. The point at which it becomes very useful is when you have programs with loops, which is why I am introducing it now.

Debugging is probably the most frustrating part of programming, but fortunately nearly all development environments, including BlueJ, provide tools to make the process less painful. These tools are called debuggers. It is a good idea to get accustomed to using a debugger now so that you will be comfortable with the debugger when you really need it, which is typically when you have a big program that is going horribly wrong. You don't want to have to learn to use the debugger when you are in crisis mode.

The most important features of a debugger are the ability to single step through your program an instruction at a time to see where something goes wrong and the ability to look at variable values as they change. Other features in any reasonable debugger include the ability to stop execution of a program in an infinite loop and the ability to set breakpoints, which will let the program execute normally until you reach a point in the program that you need to inspect in detail. BlueJ supports all of these and is easy to use.

I'll introduce the debugger through an example program that is initially incorrect and needs fixing.

11.7.1 The program to debug

The program that is shown on the following page is supposed to sum the positive odd integers from 1 to n, where n is an int value that is set when it is initialized. It has a method called oddSum(), which is called from the main() method, and this does the work of computing the sum.

```java
public class TestoddSum
// incorrect program - used to demo the debugger
{
    public static int oddSum(int n)
    {
        int sum = 0,
            i = 1;

        while (i < n)
        {
            sum += i;
            i += 2;
        }

        return sum;
    }

    public static void main()
    {
        int n = 5;
        System.out.format("Sum of odds 1 to %d is %d%n", n, oddSum(n));
    }
}
```

As long as i is less than n, the program will add i to sum and then add two to i. If I now run this program, I get the output:

```
Sum of odds 1 to 5 is 4
```

when I was hoping to be told that 1 + 3 + 5 was 9. So obviously I have made a mistake in my program, presumably somewhere in the loop. At this point it is usually easier to use the debugger to see what has gone wrong as compared to trying to read carefully through the code. I'll start by setting a breakpoint.

11.7.2 Setting a breakpoint

One of the most common actions when using a debugger is to set a breakpoint. This is a point in the program where you want execution to be suspended so that you can see what is happening then. For example, say when your program terminates you have found that a variable named x has an incorrect value, and you want to find where things went wrong so that you can correct your program. You might set breakpoints at various places in the program and start execution. When the first breakpoint is reached, execution will be suspended and you can inspect the value of x. If everything is all right so far, resume execution and then Java will continue to the next breakpoint.

With BlueJ setting a breakpoint is easy. In my sample program it seems reasonable to want to look at what is going on with the values of the variables each time that the while loop is entered and the condition (i < n) is checked. To do this click in the narrow vertical bar to the left of that line in the code window and a stop sign will be placed there.

Now run the program as usual. It will run until that line is reached and will then stop and bring up the BlueJ debug window:

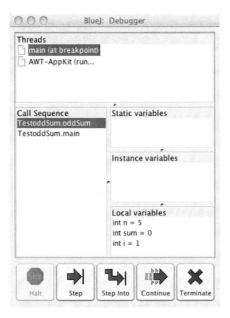

This lists the values of the three variables n, sum, and i. So far everything looks all right, so click the Continue button and BlueJ will continue execution until it gets back to this breakpoint again. This time it will show n = 5, sum = 1, and i = 3. Hit Continue again and it will show n = 5, sum = 4, and i = 5. If you hit Continue again, the program will output Sum of odds 1 to 5 is 4, and will then terminate without coming back to this statement.

This should give enough information to tell what went wrong. When i was 5, it still hadn't been added into sum, but the test (i < n) failed because both i and n had the value 5 at that point, which terminated the while loop prematurely.

11.7.3 Single step

Single stepping is the second most important feature in any debugger. I'll introduce it by making a change to my sample program (still incorrect) and show how single stepping makes it easy to fix.

There are a number of ways to do fix the problem that I found in the last section. One atempt could be to switch the order of the two statements in the loop so that first it increases the value of i by two and then adds that value into sum. This still gets the value wrong, because it outputs that the sum is 8 instead of 9. To see what is going on, rerun the program with the same breakpoint, but now when it stops at the `while` loop, hit the `Step` button a couple of times. This will move forward through the code an instruction at a time. After two steps the current line will be designated with an arrow as in:

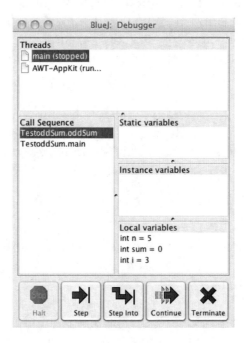

and the debug window will contain:

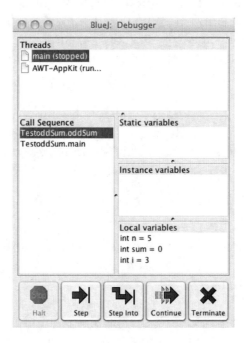

Now it is clear that I am adding 3 into `sum` when it still has the value 0, and I should have initialized it with 1, not 0, if I was going to use this loop. So make these changes, giving the program:

```java
public class TestoddSum
{
    public static int oddSum(int n)
    {
        int sum = 1,
            i = 1;

        while (i < n)
        {
            i += 2;
            sum += i;
        }

        return sum;
    }

    public static void main()
    {
        int n = 5;
        System.out.println("Sum of odds 1 to " + n + " is " + oddSum(n));
    }
}
```

Now the program will work well for any positive odd value of n. It isn't robust, which means that it does strange things if you give n a negative value (the sum will always be 1) or an even value, but that is easily fixed with an `if` statement.

11.7.4 Step into

The debug window has two `Step` buttons, `Step`, and `Step Into`. `Step` moves forward an instruction at a time, but if there is a method call it stays at its current level and doesn't drop into the method. E.g. if you put a breakpoint stop sign on the instruction `int n = 5;` in the `main()` method and start stepping when you get there it will just step through the `println()` call without ever going into `oddSum()`. If you want it to delve into called methods like this one, use `Step Into` instead of `Step`.

11.7.5 Summary and debugging recommendation

You probably could have found the errors in this program without using the debugger, but it is best to get into the habit of always using it except for the most obvious of errors. Many programmers only learn to use their debuggers when they are in a deadline crisis, find that the learning curve is too high at that point, and so are forced to keep trying to hack their way through finding the error. If you make using the debugger part of your standard procedure whenever you learn a new language or programming environment, then your life down the line will be much easier. Some debuggers can be used in a lot of programming environments. For example, the powerful Gnu Project gdb debugger can be run on all usual Windows and Unix/Linux systems and under a large number of programming languages. I recommend starting with the simple but effective BlueJ debugger for your Java programs and then later moving on to a much more powerful debugger like gdb.

11.8 Exercises

General questions

1. In the BlueJ debugger explain the difference between Step and Step Into. What do Continue and Terminate do? How do you set a breakpoint?

2. If you have a loop where, if the control codition is initially false, you want to do nothing, is a while loop or a do-while loop likely to be the better choice?

3. What will be output by the following code segment?

```
int x = 2;
for (int i = 0; i < 3; i++)
    x += 2 * i;
System.out.format("x: %d%n", x);
```

4. Give a while loop that is equivalent to the following for loop:

```
for (int i = 0; i < 3; i++)
    x += 2 * i;
```

5. Give a for loop that is equivalent to the following while loop:

```
int j = 1;
while (j <= 5)
{
    System.out.format("%d, ", j);
    j += 2;
}
System.out.println("");
```

6. What will be output by the while loop in Question 5, above?

7. Consider the following for loop:

```
for (int i = 0; i < n; i += i + 1)
{
    System.out.println(i);
    i = 2 * i;
}
```

What will be output by the loop if n is 7? Write the equivalent `while` loop. Is there any reason to prefer one loop over the other?

8. Why is it better to use a debugger as compared to just putting in a set of `System.out.println()` statements that let you see what is going on as the program executes?

9. If you know that there is an error in a section of your program, but you're not exactly sure in which line the problem arises, how would you use a combination of a breakpoint and the `Step` or `Step Into` instruction to help you find the problem?

In-lab programs

1. Type the program that I gave in Section 11.7.2 into BlueJ and play with it under the debugger. Set breakpoints, single step, and step into the code until you are comfortable with using the debugger and believe that you understand it sufficiently well so that you will use it again in the future.

2. Implement a class called `LoopTest` that has methods that test different looping methods. `LoopTest` will have no constructor or instance fields but will just have static methods that test loops that can be called from a separate `main()` (or other) method. For this in-lab write one method `public static void forTest(int n)`, which uses a `for` loop and input dialog boxes to input n double values and output the average of the n numbers with 2 decimal point precision to standard output. E.g., if n is 5 and the five double values are 1.7, -3.0, 2.5, 3.123, and 7.1234 then the method will output exactly: `The average of 1.7, -3.0, 2.5, 3.123, 7.1234, is 2.29.`

139

Out-lab programs

1. Type in the following class so that you can gain experience with the BlueJ debugger:

```java
public class DebugClass
{
    public static double second(double[] myArray)
    // supposed to find second largest value in a 1D array
    {
        double big = -1.0,
               next = -2.0;
        for (int i = 0; i < myArray.length; i++)
        {
            if (myArray[i] > big)
            {
                big = myArray[i];
                next = big;
            }
            if (myArray[i] < big && myArray[i] > next)
                next = myArray[i];
        }
        return next;
    }

    public static void main()
    {
        // first part is supposed to compute six powers of 2
        int[] weird = {1, 2, 3, 4, 5, 6};
        for (int i = 0; i < weird.length; i++)
            weird[i + 1] = 2 * weird[i];

        for (int i = 0; i < 6; i++)
            System.out.format("weird[%d] is %d%n", i, weird[i]);

        // now call the method to find the second largest value
        double[] weirder = {1.0, 3.0, 5.0, -2.0, 5.0, 3.0};
        System.out.format("Second largest is %.2f%n", second(weirder));
    }
}
```

Throughout this question use the debugger even if you can see the problem without it. When you first run this there should be an exception. Use the debugger to find where that occurs and fix it. Now there should be an incorrect value for second(). Again chase the problem down with the debugger. Now try using the array {1.0, 3.0, 5.0, -2.0, 5.0, 3.0}. Does your program correctly output 5.0 from second()? If not, get back to the debugger. As you use the debugger write down what you did in a short report.

2. Add a method public static double whileTest() to LoopTest from the in-lab that uses a Scanner and a while loop to input positive double values until a -1.0 is input as a trailer. It then returns the largest value from the list of inputs.

140

3. Add a new class called IntIntDouble to LoopTest that has three instance
    fields named int1, int2, and double1, with the obvious types. The
    constructor sets these three values and the class has three methods,
    getInt1(), getInt2(), and getDouble1() that return the values of these
    three fields.

4. Add a method public static IntIntDouble doWhileTest() to LoopTest
    that inputs positive int values with a trailer value of -1, similar to the way in
    which double values were entered in whileTest(), above. The method will
    return an IntIntDouble object where int1 is the largest value in the input
    list, int2 is the second largest, and double1 is the average of the entered
    values. This method must use a do-while to input the values.

Chapter 12. 1D Arrays

12.1 Introduction

Most computer programs deal with large amounts of data. If the data are homogeneous, which means that they are all of the same type, then they will usually be stored in arrays. In Java there will be two kinds of list structures, called *arrays* and *array lists*. Both of them let you group information on a large number of objects; the difference is that array lists are more flexible while arrays, because of their reduced flexibility, are more efficient to implement.

We could, for example, have a class list consisting of student objects, which we'll create at the beginning of the semester and then use to record scores, or whatever, during the semester. The problem with this is that, when some students add the course late or drop the course, we won't be able to handle them easily since the size of the array isn't allowed to change. With an array list there are methods to add and delete student objects, as needed, and so they would be the structure that we would use for this problem. An alternative choice would be to have an array that was at least as large as the maximum number of students who could register for the class, and then leave some of it unused most of the time.

In this chapter I'll only be looking at simple 1D lists of values, not 2D matrices or higher dimension structures. They will be covered in Chapter 14.

12.2 Simple Arrays

Arrays are *static* and *homogeneous*. Static means that, when you create the array, you set its size, which never changes after that. Homogeneous means that each element of the array contains the same kind of object (for example, a student record, an int[36], or a Player object).

Say we want to create two arrays, an array of 75 StudentRecord objects named cs160 and an array of eight ints named intArr. To do this we'll use:

```
StudentRecord[] cs160 = new StudentRecord[75];
int [] intArr = new int[8];
```

---

[36] Technically this is a bit sloppy because the eight primitive types aren't objects, but ignore that because it gets tedious to keep saying "object or primitive type" when referring to array types. However, when we get to array lists, we'll find that the distinction is important.

The names `cs160` and `intArr` then become references to the arrays in memory, just as when we created any other object. So, for example, `intArr` will reference an object with type `int[]` and after we've made a number of assignments to values in the array, we'll have something that looks like:

intArr[0]	5
intArr[1]	7
intArr[2]	undefined
intArr[3]	-4
intArr[4]	-4
intArr[5]	0
intArr[6]	3
intArr[7]	6

I'm assuming here that we've assigned values to seven of the array elements, as shown, and that one element, `intArr[2]`, hasn't had a value assigned to it yet, and so it is still undefined.

The array will be stored in contiguous memory locations and so, for example, `intArr[2]` will be in four bytes of memory, and the following four bytes will contain `intArr[3]`.

Note the names of the eight elements in the array `intArr`. They are `intArr[0]`. `intArr[1]`, ..., `intarr[7]`. This will always be true in Java, and so, for example, the 75 elements of `cs160`, as defined above, will be `cs160[0]` to `cs160[74]`. It is critical to remember that indexing starts at 0, so the first element is in position 0, the second in position 1, and so on. If you try to access, say, `intArr[8]` or `intArr[23]`, then an exception (error) will be thrown by Java.

Now say that we want to work with this array. Consider the following code segment:

```
double[] demoArray = new double[5];

System.out.format("demoArray has %d elements%n", demoArray.length);

for (int i = 0; i < 5; i++)
    demoArray[i] = i * i + i / 3.0;
demoArray[3] += demoArray[2];

System.out.format("The array contains: ");
for (int i = 0; i < demoArray.length; i++)
    System.out.format("%.2f, ", demoArray[i]);
System.out.format("%n");
```

This will output:

```
demoArray has 5 elements
The array contains: 0.00, 1.33, 4.67, 14.67, 17.33,
```

Looking at this in some detail:

- Line 1 declares an array called demoArray of five doubles.
- Line 2 uses the method length to return the length of the array, and otherwise doesn't have anything new.
- Lines 3 and 4 are a simple for loop, which assigns i * i + i * 3.0 to array element i, where i goes from 0 to 4. So the five values in the array to two decimal places are now 0.00 for position 0, 1.33 for position 1, 4.67 for position 2, 10.00 for position 3, and 17.33 for position 4.
- In line 5 I add 4.67 (the value in demoArray[2]) to demoArray[3] to make it 14.67.
- Lines 6, 7, 8, and 9 print out the value of the array in the format shown. Note that in the for loop I've now used i < demoArray.length instead of the i < 5 that I used in the first for loop. This is much better programming because if, for example, I were to later change the size of the array, I might forget to change one of these termination checks. This way I'm safe.

Some things to remember:

- To declare an array named demo of objects from the class DemoClass use DemoClass[] demo = new DemoClass[numElements];
- To find the number of elements in demo use demo.length, which returns an int.
- The elements of demo are called demo[0], demo[1], demo[2], ... demo[demo.length – 1]. 0, 1, ... demo.length – 1 are called the subscripts of the array.
- To write the header for a for loop to access each element of demo use for (int i = 0; i < demo.length; i++)

A common error is to try to access the elements of the array whose index is the number of elements in the array. So, for example, demo[demo.length] will always cause an exception because the last element is demo[demo.length – 1];

12.3 An Array Example: Saving Primes

Consider the following problem: The user will input a positive integer into *n*, and then they want us to create an array with *n* elements and use it to store the first *n* primes, starting at *2*. We'll then output these primes. I'll do this by implementing a boolean method called isprime, which will determine whether or not its argument is a prime. One solution to this problem is:

```
public class Testit
{
    public static boolean isprime(int n)
    {
        boolean retval = true;   // a number is a prime until a
                                 // factor is found
        double epsilon = 0.000001;

        for (int i = 2; i <= Math.sqrt(n) + epsilon; i++)
            if (n % i == 0)    // now we've found a factor
                retval = false;

        return retval;
    }

    public static void main()
    {
        Scanner in = new Scanner(System.in);

        System.out.println("Enter number of primes needed");
        int n = in.nextInt();
        int[] primes = new int[n];
        int index = 0,  // next available array location
            value = 2;  // next value to check for primality
        do
        {
            if (isprime(value))
            {
                primes[index] = value;
                index++;
            }
            value++;
        } while (index < primes.length);

        for (int i = 0; i < primes.length; i++)
            System.out.format("Next prime is %2d%n", primes[i]);
    }
}
```

This program will give rise to sessions like:

```
Enter number of primes needed
11
Next prime is  2
Next prime is  3
Next prime is  5
Next prime is  7
Next prime is 11
Next prime is 13
Next prime is 17
Next prime is 19
Next prime is 23
Next prime is 29
Next prime is 31
```

I've packaged everything into a class called Testit. The method isprime is static because here it is called from within a static method, main.

First let's look at isprime. If its parameter, n, isn't a prime, then it must have some integer factor bigger than 1. We don't need to look past its square root, because if, for example, n is equal to $a * b$, then at least one of a and b can't be bigger than n's square root. So here I'm checking to see whether it is divisible by 2, 3, 4, ... up to its

146

square root, by checking to see whether its remainder when divided by those values is equal to zero. I start with `retval = true;` and only change it to `false` if I find a factor of *n*. Then I return `retval`.

I could have approximately doubled the speed of `isprime` for large *n* by replacing it with

```
public static boolean isprime(int n)
{
    boolean retval = true;
    double epsilon = 0.000001;

    if (n == 2)
        retval = true;
    else if (n % 2 == 0)
        retval = false;
    else
        for (int i = 3; i <= Math.sqrt(n) + epsilon; i += 2)
            if (n % i == 0)
                retval = false;

    return retval;
}
```

where I handle all potential even number factors immediately and then only have to be concerned with odd number factors. I could have modified this further by taking care of 3 and divisibility by 3 as special cases as well, and so on, but I won't. If I were going to do this correctly, I'd just test for divisibility by other primes between 2 and $\sqrt{n}$, but I want to keep things relatively simple here.

Now let's look at the main method where I am working with arrays. I input a value, n, which is the number of primes that the user wants, using the usual prompt and `Scanner` system. Then an array of size n is created to hold the primes. Then I have a `do-while` loop, which starts at 2 and checks whether 2, 3, 4, ..., are primes, saving these values in `value`, which is incremented at the end of each loop. Whenever it finds a prime, it saves it in the next available element of the array, which is element `index`. `index` is initialized to zero, and each time a prime is placed in the array `index` is then incremented. Once the array is full, which is when `index` is equal to the length of the array, the `while` check fails and we quit the loop.

Finally I print out the elements in the array with a `for` loop.

Now I'll look at a couple of improvements.

The code, which places a new prime in the array and then increments `index`, currently is:

```
if (isprime(value))
{
    primes[index] = value;
    index++;
}
```

A standard programming technique is to use the ++ operator as soon as the location has been computed by replacing this with:

```
if (isprime(value))
    primes[index++] = value;
```

which is a bit more concise.

Another place where we can gain readability is in the for loop, which currently is:

```
for (int i = 0; i < primes.length; i++)
    System.out.format("Next prime is %2d%n", primes[i]);
```

We can replace this with the foreach loop (which will be described in Section 12.5):

```
for (int val : primes)
    System.out.format("Next prime is %2d%n", val);
```

The for line can be read as "for each value (which I'll call val) in the array named primes perform the statement (or block of statements) that follows."

12.4 Initializing 1D Arrays

Say that we have a 1D array named firstInts of ints, with 10 elements, which we want to initialize to the first 10 integers, stating at 1. So we want firstInts[0] to contain 1, firstInts[1] to contain 2, ..., firstInts[9] to contain 10.

The ugliest way to set up this array would be:

```
int[] firstInts = new int[10];
firstInts[0] = 1;
firstInts[1] = 2;
firstInts[2] = 3;
firstInts[3] = 4;
firstInts[4] = 5;
firstInts[5] = 6;
firstInts[6] = 7;
firstInts[7] = 8;
firstInts[8] = 9;
firstInts[9] = 10;
```

Somewhat better would be to use:

```
int[] firstInts = new int[10];
for (int i = 0; i < firstInts.length; i++)
    firstInts[i] = i + 1;
```

Even better, if you know the values that you want in a small array, is to use:

```
int firstInts = {1, 2, 3, 4, 5, 6, 7, 8, 9, 10};
```

Here the number of values between the braces specifies the length of the array, and the initial value of each element is given. For example, `firstInts[3]` will be 4. When it can be used, this is the approach that is always taken for putting initial values into an array because it takes less space and is much more readable.

12.5 The `foreach` Statement

The `foreach` statement is based, as I mentioned in the previous chapter on looping structures, on the `foreach` statement loved by Perl programmers. In Java it uses the familiar `for` keyword and has one of two forms:

```
for (type var : arrayname)
    statement or block of statements

for (var : arrayname)
    statement or block of statements.
```

The difference is only whether or not `var` is declared to be local to these statements, and in general the first version is preferred. The type of `var` must be the same as the array element type, and the meaning of the loop is "for each value, which I'll name `var`, in the array, do the statement(s) in the loop body.

When it can be used, it is very concise, and very readable, and so it should be used whenever possible.

For example, consider the two loops below, which will both compute the sum of the elements in the given array:

```
double[] numbers = {3.0, 2.6, -1.5, 2.7, 1.8, 0.2, -11.6};
double sum1 = 0.0,  // sum for for loop
       sum2 = 0.0;  // sum for foreach loop

for (int i = 0; i < numbers.length; i++)
    sum1 += numbers[i];

for (double value : numbers)
    sum2 += value;
```

The `foreach` was only added to Java in Java 5, so it isn't supported in outdated versions of the language.

149

12.6 Exercises

General questions

1. A ten-element array named oddnums contains the first ten positive odd integers, 1, 3, ... 19. (a) Declare the array and initialize it using a for loop. (b) Declare the array and initialize it using a foreach loop. (c) Declare the array and initialize it in the declaration (this is the preferred approach).

2. If the array oddnums is declared as described in question 1, above, what is the value of oddnums[1]? What is the value of oddnums[10]?

3. Say that I wanted to declare another array named oddnums2 that contained the first thousand odd numbers. Of the three initialization methods used in question 1, above, which would be the worst approach to use?

4. If I have the declaration double[] quest4 = {1.0, 2.0, 3.0, 5.0, 7.0, 11.0}; , (a) how many elements will there be in quest4? (b) what is the value of quest4[4]?

5. If quest4 is defined as in question 4, and I run the code:

```
for (int i = 1; i < quest4.length; i++)
    quest4[i] = 1 + quest4[i - 1];
```

what will be the six values in quest4?

6. If the code in the last question were changed to:

```
for (int i = 1; i < quest4.length - 1; i++)
    quest4[i] = 2 * quest4[i - 1];
```

what would the values be now?

7. What will be output by the following code segment?

```
int[] fred = new int[7];
fred[2] = 7;
fred[1] = fred[2] - 4;
fred[3] = 2;
fred[fred[1]] = 4;
System.out.format("%d %d %d%n", fred[1], fred[2], fred[3]);
```

8. If the line fred[7] = 2 * fred[1]; were added to the end of the code segment in Question 7, what would happen?

150

9. Declare a four-element array of doubles called `jane` and give it the initial values 3.0, -2.5, 1.3, and 0.5.

In-lab programs

1. Write and test a method `public int[] getVector()` which uses a Scanner object to input a value length which gives the length of a 1D array. Then read `length int` values into an array, which is returned from the method. Test your method and output the array.

2. Write a method `public double dotProduct(double[] vectorA, double[] vectorB)` that returns the dot product of the two vectors, which is the sum of the products of all pairs of values from the two arrays. E.g., `dotProduct({3, 1, 0, 2, -1}, {2, 0, 1, 1, 2})` is 3 * 2 + 1 * 0 + 0 * 1 + 2 * 1 + -1 * 2, which is 6. Give an error message if the the arrays don't have the same length.

3. Write and test a method `public static int[3] top3(int[] myArray)` that returns a three element array containing the three largest values in `myArray`.

Out-lab programs

1. Write and test a method `public static void reverse(int[] myArray)` which reverses the values in the array. Do this two ways, (a) by working from both ends exchanging values until it meets in the middle, and (b) by copying values left to right from the array into a temporary array right to left, and then copying the values in the temporary array back into the original. Your tests should include both odd and even length arrays.

2. Write and test a method `public static int[3] top3(int[] myArray)` that returns a three element array containing the three largest values in `myArray`.

3. Build a class Team with two instance fields, int arrSize and Player[] Team, where Player is the class defined in Chapter 2. The value for arrSize is set by the constructor, and the array size is set to that value. The method printTeam outputs the name and batting average for each player on the team, with one player per line.

Chapter 13. Array Lists

13.1 Introduction

Array Lists are dynamic homogeneous collections of objects, as compared to arrays that, as we have seen, are static and homogeneous. So the difference is that they are dynamic, not static. What this means is that with arrays the size of the array is fixed when it is created, whereas array lists start off empty when they are created and then during execution of the program values can be added to the list or deleted from the list at any time. So the size of the list will change significantly during execution. A typical use of an array list is to create it and then add the initial collection of objects as new elements. After that objects will be added to, or deleted from, the array list.

Consider the student records for a class. At the beginning of the semester the student records for all of the students who have registered for the course will be put into the array list. Then as the semester progresses some students will drop and others will do late adds, and as this happens, the number of elements in the array list will decrease and increase.

13.2 Array List Implementation Details

I'll introduce array lists through an example program, and will then get into the details of what is going on. However, first a few basics:

- The number of elements in an array list named `arrlist` can be found using `arrlist.size()`. Note that this is different from arrays, which use `arr.length`, so this is not only a different name but also one uses parentheses while the other doesn't.
- Indexing in an array list begins at 0, as it does for arrays, so the elements of the array list above are numbered from 0 to `arrlist.size() - 1`.
- Array lists can only have elements that are objects, which means that they cannot directly contain any of the eight primitive types (the six numeric types, `char`, and `boolean`). To get around this, recent versions of Java have included wrapper classes for these eight types, which let you use them in array lists. I'll demonstrate these in Section 13.5.
- To get the value of, say, the fifth element of the array list `arrlist`, you have to use `arrlist.get(4)`. That is, there is no equivalent of the `[4]` notation used for arrays, but instead you use the `get()` method that is defined in the `ArrayList` class.

153

- Similarly, the set() method is used to change the value of an element, and so to change the value of, say, the fifth element of the array list `arrlist`, you have to use `arrlist.set(4)`.
- `ArrayList` is a Java class that is in `java.util.ArrayList`. So to use one or more array lists in your programs you need to either `import java.util.*;` or `import java.util.ArrayList;`.

There are a large number of methods provided in the `ArrayList` class that let you manipulate array lists. Look at the online Java documentation to see them all. I'll first describe those that you can expect to use most often. In the examples below I'll assume that I have declared an array list called example whose members are of type T, where T is a class. To do this declaration the format is:

```
ArrayList<T> example = new ArrayList<T>();
```

which will create an empty array list as described above. The following methods are those that you will most often use. They assume that value is an object of type `T` and that index is an `int`.

`example.size()`: returns the number of elements in the array list, which will be 0 when it is created.
`example.add(value)`: adds a new element to the end of the array list with the specified value.
`example.add(index, value)`: will insert the new element into the array list at the specified index position. All elements that were previously at that index position or higher will be pushed down so that their index positions are all increased by 1.
`example.remove(index)`: removes the element at the specified index position and so any later elements will be shifted up. The method also returns the value of the removed list element.
`example.clear()`: removes all elements from the list.

For example, consider the following code segment. Don't worry about why I'm declaring the list with type Integer instead of int – I'll get to that later.

```
ArrayList<Integer> numbers = new ArrayList<Integer>();
numbers.add(5);
numbers.add(3);
numbers.add(-2);
// list now contains 5, 3, and -2 in that order
numbers.add(1, 2)  // insert 2 into index 1 and shift any others
// list now contains 5, 2, 3, and -2 in that order
numbers.remove(2)  // remove value at index 2
// list now contains 5, 2, and -2 in that order
```

154

13.3 An Array List Example

As an example of an array list in action I'll use the student record problem that I discussed above. This will take three class definitions:

- Class StudentRecord: This will define the StudentRecord type for an individual student record. The instance fields will be two strings for student name and major and a double for the student's current GPA. Methods will be getGPA() to find a student's GPA, changeGPA(newGPA) to change it, and printRecord() to print the student's name, major, and GPA.
- Class StudentDB: This will use an array list to store a database of student records for a class. The instance field will be the array list, the constructor won't have to do anything, and the methods will be readAndAddRecord() to read in a student record from the input and add it to the class database, printCourse() to output the records for all of the students in the class, and methods to manipulate the list.
- Class UnitTest: Will create a DB for a class called cs160, and will show the methods used to work with array lists.

13.3.1 Class StudentRecord

```
public class StudentRecord
{
    // instance fields
    private String name;
    private String major;
    private double gpa;

    // Constructor for objects of class StudentRecord
    public StudentRecord(String in_name, String in_major,
                         double in_gpa)
    {
        // initialize instance fields
        name = in_name;
        major = in_major.toUpperCase(); // store major in upper case
        gpa = in_gpa;
    }

    public double getgpa()
    {
        return gpa;
    }

    public void changeGPA(double newGPA)
    {
        gpa = newGPA;
    }

    public void printRecord()
    {
        System.out.format("Name: %s, major: %s, GPA: %4.2f%n",
                          name, major, gpa);
    }
}
```

There is nothing new in this class.

13.3.2 Class StudentDB

```java
import java.util.*;
public class StudentDB
{
    private ArrayList<StudentRecord> studentDB =
                        new ArrayList<StudentRecord>();
    private static Scanner in = new Scanner(System.in);

    public StudentDB()
    {
        // nothing needs to be done in the constructor
    }

    public void readAndAddRecord(){
    // read in a new record and add to the list
        String first, last, name, major;
        double gpa;
        System.out.print("Enter a student record ");
        System.out.println("(first, last, major, gpa)");
        first = in.next();  // get first and last names, then
        last = in.next();    // use format to join them into name
        name = String.format("%s %s", first, last);
        major = in.next();
        gpa = in.nextDouble();
        studentDB.add(new StudentRecord(name, major, gpa));
    }

    public void printCourse()
    // output all of the student records in a course
    {
        for (StudentRecord student : studentDB)
            student.printRecord();
    }

    public StudentRecord remove(int index)
    // Remove the record at a specified index and return its value
    {
        return studentDB.remove(index);
    }

    public void add(int index, StudentRecord newstudent)
    // insert a new record at the specified location
    {
        studentDB.add(index, newstudent);
    }

    public void set(int index, StudentRecord newstudent)
    // change the value at the specified location to the new record
    {
        studentDB.set(index, newstudent);
    }

    public StudentRecord get(int index)
    // return the record stored at the specified location
    {
        return studentDB.get(index);
    }
}
```

Read through this carefully. The array list instance field is `private`, as usual, so to modify it I need `set()`, `get()`, `insert()`, and `remove()` methods which just call on the standard array list methods so that I can access the array list from outside the class. Other that that there shouldn't be any surprises in the code. As usual I've removed all of the Javadocs comments to save space.

13.3.3 Class UnitTest

To test the classes I used the following unit test in a `main()` method:

```
public class UnitTest
{
    public static void main()
    {
        StudentDB cs160 = new StudentDB();

        for (int i = 1; i <= 4; i++)
            cs160.readAndAddRecord();
        System.out.format("%nInitial class roll%n");
        cs160.printCourse();

        StudentRecord outval;
        System.out.format("%nDelete second record. Record is:%n");
        outval = cs160.remove(1);
        outval.printRecord();
        System.out.format("%nCourse now contains:%n");
        cs160.printCourse();

        StudentRecord
            fred = new StudentRecord("Fred Smith", "cs", 2.5),
        System.out.format("%nInsert fred's record after first%n");
        System.out.format("& change the third to jane's record%n");
        cs160.add(1, fred);
        cs160.set(2, new StudentRecord("Jane Jones", "MB", 3.5));
        cs160.printCourse();

        System.out.format("%nPrint out the second record%n");
        temp = cs160.get(1);
        temp.printRecord();
    }
}
```

The first line sets up a `StudentDB` array list for the course cs160.

The second group of statements prompts for four student records and inputs them in a for loop using our `readAndAddRecord()` method. Then it prints out the current four elements.

The third group uses add() to add one student's record (`Fred Smith`) and set() to change another record to `Jane Jones`' record. I've done this in two ways, by assigning one record to a variable and then using that and by putting `Jane Jones`' record in directly.

The final group shows that an individual record can be retrieved.

13.3.4 Class program output

```
Enter a student record (first, last, major, gpa)
John Smith cs 2.8
Enter a student record (first, last, major, gpa)
Jane Jones
ECE
3.4
Enter a student record (first, last, major, gpa)
Mick Jagger MUS 4.0
Enter a student record (first, last, major, gpa)
Petronella Pulsford MTA 3.2

Initial class roll
Name: John Smith, major: CS, GPA: 2.80
Name: Jane Jones, major: ECE, GPA: 3.40
Name: Mick Jagger, major: MUS, GPA: 4.00
Name: Petronella Pulsford, major: MTA, GPA: 3.20

Delete the second record
Name: John Smith, major: CS, GPA: 2.80
Name: Mick Jagger, major: MUS, GPA: 4.00
Name: Petronella Pulsford, major: MTA, GPA: 3.20

Insert fred's record after the first
and change the third entry to jane's record
Name: John Smith, major: CS, GPA: 2.80
Name: Fred Smith, major: CS, GPA: 2.50
Name: Jane Jones, major: VMB, GPA: 3.50
Name: Petronella Pulsford, major: MTA, GPA: 3.20

Print out the second record
Name: Fred Smith, major: CS, GPA: 2.50
```

When I run the program I get the output above. My inputs to the program are shown in **bold**. Nothing here should be a surprise–all of the outputs are doing what they are supposed to.

13.4 Converting from an Array List to a 1D Array

`listname.toArray()` returns an array of type `ClassName[]`, which is created from the elements of the array list. This is usually used if the list is initially dynamic, with objects being added and deleted, but then becomes stable with a fixed number of elements. Array manipulations are more efficient than array list manipulations, and so converting the array list to an array once it has been stabilized will make subsequent operations more efficient. The `Array` class doesn't have a comparable `toListArray()` method to go back later if needed, but that is trivial to implement with a foreach loop.

For more details on all of these methods and for information on a few other methods that are less commonly used, see the Java 6 documentation.

13.5 Wrapping Primitive Types in Array Lists

As I discussed earlier, array lists can only contain objects. Since the eight primitive types (`byte`, `short`, `int`, `long`, `float`, `double`, `char`, and `boolean`) aren't objects, this causes problems if we want an array list of, say, `int`s. Getting around this was annoyingly difficult in early versions of Java, but since Java 5 it has been easy. The solution is through a concept called a wrapper class combined with boxing and unboxing. Since Java 5, boxing and unboxing are done automatically, without the user having to do anything, and so boxing is now called autoboxing or auto-boxing.

The idea of a wrapper class is that since, for example, a `double` isn't an object, then Java provides a class called `Double` that contains a `double`, and then these objects can be in array lists. So you take, say, a `double`, and wrap it up in a box and call the box a `Double`. When you need it as a `double`, then you take it out of this box again. This is called wrapping, boxing, and unboxing. There are eight wrapper classes in Java corresponding to the eight primitive types. They are:

Wrapper Class	Contained type
Byte	byte
Short	short
Integer	int
Long	long
Float	float
Double	double
Character	char
Boolean	boolean

Java likes to have class names that are complete words, and so while six of the classes correspond to the types of the wrapped type (with the first letter changed to uppercase), in the two cases where the wrapped types are abbreviations (`int` and `char`) the wrapper type is given a full name (`Integer` and `Character`). I find this annoying and wish that the class designers had used `Int` and `Char` for the wrapper classes, but we are stuck with their decision.

Using wrapper classes is now so easy that in most cases the programmer doesn't need to know what is going on under the hood. If I want an array list of numbers (or `char`s or `boolean`s), I declare the list using the wrapper type name. So if, for example, I want an array list named `doublelist` of `double`s, then I declare

```
ArrayList<Double> doubleList = new ArrayList<Double>();
```

and everything will work. We can, for example, say `doubleList.add(3.5)` and automatically `3.5` will be boxed into a `Double`, which will then be added to the array list. If this value happens to be stored in element numbered `27` in the array list and if I then say

```
double var = 2 * doubleList.get(27);
```

then all that programmers usually care about is that `var` gets the value `7.0` assigned to it. What has actually happened is more complicated; the `get` method has returned the `Double 3.5`, which is a `double` in a box, not a `double`. However, when Java sees that a number is needed, it unboxes it, which means that the double `3.5` is multiplied by `2` to get the double `7.0` as its value.

So while a lot is going on when we use these wrapper classes, we can now ignore everything complex, because Java now does all of the conversions automatically without the user needing to know what has just been done for them.

We have seen these wrapper classes before, when doing input from a dialog box. That input came in as a string, so then if, for example, we wanted a `double`, we had to use `Double.parseDouble(str)` to convert the incoming string `str` to a `double`.

13.6 Exercises

General questions

1. Give the decaration for an array list of `String` values named `stringList`.

2. Can I initialize `sringList` as described in Question 1 to contain the two strings `Denbigh` and `Starkey` in its declaration? If I can, show how. If I cannot, then show the declaration and how I should then add these two values to the array list?

3. Give the declaration for an array list named `intList` that will contain `int` values.

4. When is a wrapper class needed?

5. How many wrapper classes are there, and what are their names?

6. What will be output by the following code segment? Be precise.

```
ArrayList<Integer> john = new ArrayList<Integer>();
john.add(2);
john.add(3);
john.add(1, 6);
john.add(7);
john.remove(2);
for (int i = 0; i < john.size(); i++)
    System.out.format("%d-", john.get(i));
System.out.println("");
```

7. In Question 6, would it have made a difference if I had replaced the `john.remove(2)` call with `john.remove((Integer) 2)`? If so, what would have been the output? To answer this it might help to look at the online ducumentation for the `ArrayList` class and look at different options for the `remove()` method.

8. Why didn't I use the following for the declaration in Question 6, above?

```
ArrayList<int> john = new ArrayList<int>();
```

In-lab programs

1. Write and test a method `public int[] listToVector(ArrayList<Integer> myList)` that takes any array list of `Integer` values and returns a 1D array of `int` values that contains the elements of the list. For example, if the array list contains `3, 5, 6, 2, -4,` and `8` then it will return a 1D `int[]` array containing these six values. The `ListArray` class provides a method that does this, but write your own instead of using it. This is a very useful method because if, for example, your data values are dynamic for a while but then become static, you use an array list as elements are added and deleted, and then convert to a 1D array for greater efficiency once the values have stabilized.

2. Similar to in-lab 1, above, but go in the opposite direction. That is, write a method `vectorToList(int[] myVector)` that returns an `Integer` array list.

Out-lab programs

1. Test the methods in in-lab 1 and 2 by putting them into a class, and then initially add elements to a list, convert to a 1D array, sort the array in increasing order, convert back to an array list, add and delete some values, and finally convert back to a 1D array, sort it, and output its values, sorted.

2. Write a method `public static double[3] top3(ArrayList<Double> myList)` that returns a 1D array containing the three largest values in the list. Your method should be able to handle and positive or negative values in the list.

3. Write a class Student whose instance fields are String name, String department, and double gradeAverage. Write another class called Course, whose only instance field is an array list of Student values. Course has three methods: register(Student newStudent) adds the student to the course, drop(Student newStudent) drops the student from the course, printGrades() prints out the grades for each student, with one student per line, with the student's name, gradeAverage, and letter grade. Letter grades are determined as A ≥ 90, B ≥ 80, C ≥ 70, D ≥ 60, F < 60. Your grade report should be nicely formatted, in clean columns. Use the length of the longest name to determine the size of its column.

4. Sort the grade report in out-lab 3, above.

Chapter 14. Multi-Dimensional Arrays

14.1 Introduction

Data often naturally fit into a matrix form, which in Java means that they should be represented as a 2D (two-dimensional) array. Sometimes higher dimensional arrays are a natural way to store information for processing. As simple examples of 2D arrays, consider the following:

- o A spreadsheet for student grades: a row for each student and a column for the student's score on each assignment. Note that this could also be considered as a 1D array of student record objects, where each object contains all of the student's scores on each assignment. However the latter approach might be much less efficient if, for example, we want to compute statistics for the class (e.g., min, max, mean, and median) for each assignment.

- o A set of simultaneous linear equations: it is common in computing to have to solve very large numbers of simultaneous equations, and they are usually represented as 2D arrays. For example, the three simultaneous equations

$$3x + 2y - z = 4.5$$
$$2.5x - y = 1.7$$
$$x + y + z = 6$$

could be represented by the matrix (2D array)

3.0	2.0	-1.0	4.5
2.5	-1.0	0.0	1.7
1.0	1.0	1.0	6.0

In this chapter I'll first describe 2D arrays, and then will extend my primary 2D example and show how it could be more naturally represented as a 3D array.

14.2 2D Arrays

As an example, take the matrix representation of the three simultaneous equations shown above. It has three rows and four columns and could be declared in Java with:

```
double[][] simul = new double[3][4];
```

and then initialized using

```
simul[0][0] = 3; simul[0][1] = 2; simul[0][2] = -1; simul[0][3] = 4.5;
simul[1][0] = 2.5; simul[1][1] = -1; simul[1][2] = 0; simul[1][3] = 1.7;
simul[2][0] = 1; simul[2][1] = 1; simul[2][2] = 1; simul[2][3] = 6;
```

Or, using a notation similar to that used for directly declaring and initializing 1D arrays we could use:

```
double[][] simul = {{3, 2, -1, 4.5},
                    {2.5, -1, 0, 1.7},
                    {1, 1, 1, 6}};
```

which is obviously much nicer.

Alternatively, although this often doesn't gain anything, we could declare and initialize three 1D arrays and then use them as in:

```
double[] row1 = {3, 2, -1, 4.5},
         row2 = {2.5, -1, 0, 1.7},
         row3 = {1, 1, 1, 6};
double[][] simul = {row1, row2, row3};
```

These examples have shown a few features of Java multi-dimensional arrays. Some of these are:

- To directly access, say, the fourth element of the second row of the array, I used simul[1][3]. So the first index (value between [and]) gives the row index and the second the column index. Also, the indexing of both dimensions begins with 0, as they did in 1D arrays, so, for example, the second row has row index 1 and the fourth column has column index 3.

- As the last declaration showed, a 2D array can always be considered as a 1D array of 1D arrays. So in that declaration simul was declared as a 2D array of doubles, and was then initialized as a 1D array with three elements, each of which was a 1D array with four double values.

- Since a 2D array in Java is just a 1D array of 1D arrays, this provides a lot of generality. In particular, as I will show later in this chapter, the number of elements in each row does not have to be constant, and so Java supports non-rectangular 2D arrays. Very few programming languages handle this as cleanly as Java does.

14.3 Nested Loops

When processing 1D arrays, nearly all programs use simple for loops. With 2D arrays we will have nested loops where the outer loop typically accesses each row of the array and the inner loop then accesses each element within that row.

Say that one wants to find the sum of all of the values in the simul array shown above. This will be done using these *nested for loops*. If we know that the array is rectangular with three rows and four columns, as shown, then one code segment to sum the 12 values is:

```
double sum = 0.0;
for (int row = 0; row < 3; row++)
    for (int column = 0; column < 4; column++)
        sum += simul[row][column];
```

You'll use this nested concept a lot, so I'll go through what is happening slowly.

1. sum is declared and initialized to zero.
2. The local variable row first gets the value 0, and then we execute its statement, which is the inner for loop. This will generate four values for column, column = 0, column = 1, column = 2, and column = 3, and each time it will add simul[row][column] to sum. So since row is 0, what will happen is that we will add first simul[0][0] to sum, then simul[0][1], then simul[0][2], then simul[0][3].
3. row next gets the value 1, and we repeat the loop that sets column to 0, 1, 2, and 3. That is, this will add simul[1][0], simul[1][1], simul[1][2], and simul[1][3] to sum.
4. Finally row is 2, which in the same way will add simul[2][0], simul[2][1], simul[2][2], and simul[2][3] to sum.

So by the time that the nested loops are complete, all of the elements of the 2D array have been added to sum. Follow this example carefully until you're sure that you understand it, because using nested loops is a critical programming skill.

14.4 2D Array Notation and Accessing Row and Column Sizes

When we were using 1D arrays, we used the method length to find the number of elements in the array. For example, if we had an array called arr, then arr.length gave us its length. Similarly with 2D arrays we often want to know how many rows it has and how many elements there are in each row. Look at the third declaration that I had for the simul 2D array:

```
       double[] row1 = {3, 2, -1, 4.5},
              row2 = {2.5, -1, 0, 1.7},
              row3 = {1, 1, 1, 6};
       double[][] simul = {row1, row2, row3};
```

This makes it very clear that `simul` is an array of three elements, each of which contains four elements. This is why a 2D array is declared as `classname[][]` to make it clear that `classname[]` is a 1D array, and then an array of its kind is `classname[][]`. This implies, correctly, that to get the number of rows in `simul`, for example, all I have to use is `simul.length`, which in this case will give me 3, and to find the number of columns all I need to use is `simul[0].length`, which will give me 4. Since this is a rectangular array where all of the rows have the same number of elements, I could use `simul[i].length` for any i between 0 and 2. This means that we can make our nested loops more stable by including terminators based on lengths. For example, the example that I gave earlier could be written better as:

```
       double sum = 0;
       for (int row = 0; row < simul.length; row++)
           for (int column = 0; column < simul[row].length; column++)
               sum += simul[row][column];
```

and this will even work correctly when there is a different number of elements in each row of the array, since the inner loop uses the row length for the current row. From now on I will always use this form for my nested loops that access all elements of an array.

14.5 2D Array Example

Assume that we have four weather station sites numbered 1, 2, 3, and 4, and we have temperature recordings at each station four times each day at 3:00 am, 9:00 am, 3:00 pm, and 9:00 pm for one week. Temperatures are in centigrade and are integers. So our data in 2D tabular form look like:

#	3	9	3	9	3	9	3	9	3	9	3	9	3	9	3	9	3	9	3	9	3	9	3	9	3	9	3	9
	a	a	p	p	a	a	p	p	a	a	p	p	a	a	p	p	a	a	p	p	a	a	p	p	a	a	p	p
1	0	5	9	1	3	8	9	2	1	4	6	2	3	8	9	4	2	7	8	3	1	4	7	5	4	7	8	3
2	1	3	7	3	4	9	9	1	0	5	7	4	2	4	4	1	3	8	9	2	1	5	6	0	3	4	5	1
3	0	4	5	5	2	6	7	1	4	8	9	2	3	6	8	5	1	7	6	0	2	4	8	7	1	3	9	2
4	4	5	4	1	3	8	6	4	5	9	7	2	4	7	9	1	2	3	2	0	0	4	5	6	2	8	9	7

Obviously this table is ugly, and as I'll show later, a 3D array is more appropriate for this problem. For now, though, I'll stick with 2D. Assume that I want two pieces of information from this table:

1. What is the average temperature (based on these four sites and the times that data was recorded) for the week?

166

2. At a specified site, what was the average temperature of the warmest day?

I'll build a class called `Temperatures`. I want it to be general and so, for any instance of `Temperatures`, I need to know how many days are recorded, and how many temperatures there are per day since I can't extract those from the array definition. I also, of course, need the 2D array of temperatures. Since these are the things that are needed to do the calculations, these will be the instance fields. I'll show my code and then discuss it. In the code I'll stub out (i.e., replace the code with a comment) the two methods and then define them later.

```java
// For an array of temperature data from multiple sites compute
// the average temperature and the hottest day average at
// a specified site.
public class Temperatures
{
    // instance fields
    private int[][] temps;          // array of temperature data
    private final int days;         // number of days of data
    private final int readsPer;     // number of readings/day/site

    /**
     * Constructor for objects of class Temperatures
     */
    public Temperatures(int[][] in_data, int in_days, int in_readsPer)
    {
        // initialise instance fields
        temps = in_data;
        days = in_days;
        readsPer = in_readsPer;
    }

    // find average temp for all sites over the time period
    public double avgTemp()
    {
        // not yet defined
    }

    // find hottest day number and avg temp for specified site
    public SiteDayAvg siteMax(int siteNum)
    {
        // not yet defined
    }
}
```

The `siteMax()` method needs to return both a day number and an average temperature for that day, and so, since it is returning both an int and a double, I've called the return value type `SiteDayAvg`, which is a simple class that I need to define.

```
// Class to hold a day number and average temperature
public class SiteDayAvg
{
    // instance fields
    private int day;
    private double temp;

    // Constructor for objects of class SiteDayAvg
    publicSiteDayAvg(int in_day, double in_temp)
    {
        // initialize instance fields
        day = in_day;
        temp = in_temp;
    }

    // return the temperature component
    public double getTemp()
    {
        return temp;
    }

    // return the day number component
    public int getDay()
    {
        return day;
    }
}
```

all of which is very standard.

Getting back to the Temperatures class, one new feature is the 2D array parameter, which passes in a reference to the array that is the actual parameter in the program that calls this class.[37]

I have two methods to solve the required tasks.

avgTemp() returns the average of all of the temperatures in the array, which in the example above is 112 values (four sites, seven days, four readings per day). It can be defined with:

```
// find average temp for all sites over the time period
public double avgTemp()
{
    int sum = 0;
    for (int i = 0; i < temps.length; i++)
        for (int j = 0; j < temps[0].length; j++)
            sum += temps[i][j];
    return (double) sum / (temps.length * temps[0].length);
}
```

The code is based on the standard nested for loops that I showed earlier for accessing all of the elements of a 2D array. To get the average temperature, I need to sum all of the temperature values and then divide that sum by the number of values.

_____

[37] C programmers will note the significant extra flexibility in Java. In C you have to specify the number of rows when using a 2D array as a parameter. In Java this information is maintained by the compiler.

Here the number of values in the array is the number of rows times the number of columns, which is temps.length * temps[0].length, so the sum of values is divided by this, with a cast to double of one of the values to avoid integer division truncation.

siteMax(int siteNum) will find the average temperature at the named site and will return two values, the number of the hottest day at the site (converted from 0, 1, 2, ... to 1, 2, 3, ... by adding 1) and the average temperature on that day. Since I need to return both an int for the day number and a double for the average temperature on that day, I've used the SiteDayAvg class that I defined above.

```
// find hottest day number and avg temp for specified site
public SiteDayAvg siteMax(int siteNum)
{
    int daySum,                         // sum of readings for a day
        maxDaySum = -274 * readsPer,    // warmest day so far, initialized
                                        // to (absolute_zero - 1) * readsPer
        maxDay,                         // day # of warmest day, 0, 1, ...
        siteIndex = siteNum - 1;        // site array subscript

    for (int day = 0; day < days; day++)
    {
        daySum = 0;
        for (int reading = 0; reading < readsPer; reading++)
            daySum += temps[siteIndex][day * readsPer + reading];
        if (daySum > maxDaySum)
        {
            maxDaySum = daySum;
            maxDay = day;
        }
    }
    return new SiteDayAvg(maxDay + 1, (double) maxDaySum / readsPer);
}
```

This method is slightly more complicated. For each day at the site it computes the sum of the daily readings and sees whether it is greater than the latest maximum value, which is stored in maxDaySum. If it is, then the value of maxDaySum is updated to this new value and the hottest day is changed to this day's subscript. Initially maxDaySum is set to an impossibly negative temperature average (a degree below absolute zero in centigrade for each recording). Finally the two returned values are one greater than maxDay (converting from 0, 1, ... subscripts to 1, 2, ... day numbers), and the average temperature for the hottest day.

Now we just need to have a unit test for these classes. I used the test program shown below, with the temperature values shown in the table at the beginning of this section. First, however, I tested it with much smaller temps arrays, which is the usual approach. Always test small first and then expand to production tests. The test class is on the next page.

In the class week is declared to be an object of class Temperatures, then week.avgTemp() calculates the value of all of the 112 temperatures in the table, and then for each of the four sites we find the hottest average day and the average temperature on that day using an object from the class SiteDayAvg and its two methods to return the day of the week and the average temperature that day.

For the initialization there was so much data that it was easiest to enter it in 1D arrays by site:

```java
public class UnitTest
{
    public static void main()
    {
        int[] site1 = {0, 5, 9, 1, 3, 8, 9, 2, 1, 4, 6, 2, 3, 8,
                       9, 4, 2, 7, 8, 3, 1, 4, 7, 5, 4, 7, 8, 3},
              site2 = {1, 3, 7, 3, 4, 9, 9, 1, 0, 5, 7, 4, 2, 4,
                       4, 1, 3, 8, 9, 2, 1, 5, 6, 0, 3, 4, 5, 1},
              site3 = {0, 4, 5, 5, 2, 6, 7, 1, 4, 8, 9, 2, 3, 6,
                       8, 5, 1, 7, 6, 0, 2, 4, 8, 7, 1, 3, 9, 2},
              site4 = {4, 5, 4, 1, 3, 8, 6, 4, 5, 9, 7, 2, 4, 7,
                       9, 1, 2, 3, 2, 0, 0, 4, 5, 6, 2, 8, 9, 7};
        int[][] temps = {site1, site2, site3, site4};

        Temperatures week = new Temperatures(temps, 7, 4);
        System.out.format("Average temp over all sites: %.3fC%n",
                       week.avgTemp());

        SiteDayAvg dayAvg; // holds a day number and day's temp
        for (int site = 1; site <= temps.length; site++)
        {
            dayAvg = week.siteMax(site);
            System.out.format("Hottest average day at site ");
            System.out.format("%d was day %d at %.3fC%n",
                           site, dayAvg.getDay(), dayAvg.getTemp())
        }
    }
}
```

The output from the program will be:

```
Average temp over all sites: 4.429C
Hottest average day at site 1 was day 4 at 6.000C
Hottest average day at site 2 was day 2 at 5.750C
Hottest average day at site 3 was day 3 at 5.750C
Hottest average day at site 4 was day 7 at 6.500C
```

14.6 Non-Rectangular Arrays

Because of the structure of Java array definitions, Java can build 2D (or higher dimension) arrays where each row of the array has a different number of values. For example, say that we have a very small bowling league team with three players numbered 0, 1, and 2, and we analyze their scores at the end of the season. They have probably played a different number of times, so we might have an array of scores that looks like

```java
int[][] scores = {{210, 149, 300, 164},
                  {131, 169, 110, 153, 200, 210},
                  {300, 171, 265, 184, 255}};
```

where player 0 has played four games, player 1 six games, and player 2 five games. The team gets free T-shirts if their team average is at least 200, so they want a program that will compute their team average score. This could be:

```
public static void main()
{
    int[][] scores = {{210, 149, 300, 164},
                      {131, 169, 110, 153, 200, 210},
                      {300, 171, 265, 184, 255}};
    int sum = 0,   // sum of all scores
    numgames = 0; // number of games played

    for (int player = 0; player < scores.length; player++)
        for (int game = 0; game < scores[player].length; game++)
        {
            sum += scores[player][game];
            numgames++;
        }

    System.out.format("Team average score is %.1f%n",
                      (double) sum / numgames);
}
```

where I've kept track of the sum of all scores in sum and the total games played in numgames, so I can compute the team average using sum / numgames, as long as I remember to cast one of them to double to avoid the integer division problem. If we run this, we'll get the output:

```
Team average score is 198.1
```

and so the team doesn't get the free T-shirts.

Note that this program is very stable under change. I could substitute in a new scores array definition for a team with hundreds of players playing many more games each, and the program would run correctly without modifications.

14.7 3D and Higher Dimension Arrays

Higher dimension arrays than just 1D and 2D are allowed in Java, although it is relatively rare to need to go to higher dimensions than 3D. So here I'll look at an example of a 3D array.

Remember our temperature definition where we had four weather station sites and generated data for seven days at four readings per day. I had the declaration in my 2D program:

```
    int[] site1 = {0, 5, 9, 1, 3, 8, 9, 2, 1, 4, 6, 2, 3, 8,
                   9, 4, 2, 7, 8, 3, 1, 4, 7, 5, 4, 7, 8, 3},
         site2 = {1, 3, 7, 3, 4, 9, 9, 1, 0, 5, 7, 4, 2, 4,
                   4, 1, 3, 8, 9, 2, 1, 5, 6, 0, 3, 4, 5, 1},
         site3 = {0, 4, 5, 5, 2, 6, 7, 1, 4, 8, 9, 2, 3, 6,
                   8, 5, 1, 7, 6, 0, 2, 4, 8, 7, 1, 3, 9, 2},
         site4 = {4, 5, 4, 1, 3, 8, 6, 4, 5, 9, 7, 2, 4, 7,
                   9, 1, 2, 3, 2, 0, 0, 4, 5, 6, 2, 8, 9, 7};
    int[][] temps = {site1, site2, site3, site4};
```

This really didn't follow the structure of the problem description because for each site we have a listing of all 28 readings, without knowing whether this is, say, seven days at four readings per day, 28 days at one reading per day, or four days at seven readings per day. As a result, when I created a Temperatures object, I had to explicitly specify the number of days and readings per day.

A better solution, which would simplify the code, would be to treat each site's readings as a 2D array where I specify the four readings for each day. Under this approach the initialization would be:

```
    int[][] site1 = {{0, 5, 9, 1}, {3, 8, 9, 2}, {1, 4, 6, 2},
                     {3, 8, 9, 4}, {2, 7, 8, 3}, {1, 4, 7, 5},
                     {4, 7, 8, 3}},
           site2 = {{1, 3, 7, 3}, {4, 9, 9, 1}, {0, 5, 7, 4},
                    {2, 4, 4, 1}, {3, 8, 9, 2}, {1, 5, 6, 0},
                    {3, 4, 5, 1}},
           site3 = {{0, 4, 5, 5}, {2, 6, 7, 1}, {4, 8, 9, 2},
                    {3, 6, 8, 5}, {1, 7, 6, 0}, {2, 4, 8, 7},
                    {1, 3, 9, 2}},
           site4 = {{4, 5, 4, 1}, {3, 8, 6, 4}, {5, 9, 7, 2},
                    {4, 7, 9, 1}, {2, 3, 2, 0}, {0, 4, 5, 6},
                    {2, 8, 9, 7}};
    int[][][] temps = {site1, site2, site3, site4};
```

making temps a 4 × 7 × 4 3D array where each of its four elements is a 7 × 4 2D array.

With this structure the user will no longer need to pass in any information when they create a Temperatures object apart from the array, because the number of sites is temps.length, the number of days is temps[i].length, and the number of readings per day is temps[i][j].length for any i and j in the appropriate ranges (for example, one can safely use 0 for both i and j).

Moving to a 3D array gives rise to slight changes in two of the three classes (the SiteDayAvg class doesn't need to change at all).

The Temperatures class, renamed to Temperatures3D, becomes:

```java
// For an array of temperature data from multiple sites compute
// the average temperature and the hottest day average at
// a specified site.
public class Temperatures3D
{
    private int[][][] temps;       // 3D array of temperature data
    private final int sites;       // number of sites
    private final int days;        // number of days
    private final int readsPer;    // number of readings per day

    // Constructor for objects of class Temperatures3D
    public Temperatures3D(int[][][] in_temps)
    {
        temps = in_temps;
        // compute sites, days, and readsPer from array definition
        sites = temps.length;
        days = temps[0].length;
        readsPer = temps[0][0].length;
    }

    // Find the average temperature at all sites for the time period
    public double avgTemp()
    {
        double sum = 0;
        for (int i = 0; i < sites; i++)
            for (int j = 0; j < days; j++)
                for (int k = 0; k < readsPer; k++)
                    sum += temps[i][j][k];
        return sum / (sites * days * readsPer);
    }

    // Find hottest day for a specified weather site
    public SiteDayAvg siteMax(int siteNum)
    {
        int daySum = 0,
            maxDaySum = -274 * 4, // absolute zero is -273C
            maxDay = 0,
            siteIndex = siteNum - 1;

        for (int day = 0; day < days; day++) {
            daySum = 0;
            for (int reading = 0; reading < readsPer; reading++)
                daySum += temps[siteIndex][day][reading];
            if (daySum > maxDaySum)
            {
                maxDaySum = daySum;
                maxDay = day;
            }
        }
        return new SiteDayAvg(maxDay + 1,
                    (double) maxDaySum / readsPer);
    }
}
```

Note that the constructor now no longer needs to be told the number of days and the number of readings per day since they can be extracted from the array structure.

So that I don't need to keep using temps[0].length for the number of days and temps[0][0].length for the number of readings per day, I pre-computed them in the constructor and saved them in variables. Once computed, their values should never change, so I have declared them as final.

One new feature is the triply nested loop, but it should be easy to trace through.

173

The `UnitTest` class now uses the `Temperatures3D` class, so it becomes:

```
public class UnitTest
{
    public static void main()
    {
        int[][] site1 = {{0, 5, 9, 1}, {3, 8, 9, 2}, {1, 4, 6, 2},
                         {3, 8, 9, 4}, {2, 7, 8, 3}, {1, 4, 7, 5},
                         {4, 7, 8, 3}},
                site2 = {{1, 3, 7, 3}, {4, 9, 9, 1}, {0, 5, 7, 4},
                         {2, 4, 4, 1}, {3, 8, 9, 2}, {1, 5, 6, 0},
                         {3, 4, 5, 1}},
                site3 = {{0, 4, 5, 5}, {2, 6, 7, 1}, {4, 8, 9, 2},
                         {3, 6, 8, 5}, {1, 7, 6, 0}, {2, 4, 8, 7},
                         {1, 3, 9, 2}},
                site4 = {{4, 5, 4, 1}, {3, 8, 6, 4}, {5, 9, 7, 2},
                         {4, 7, 9, 1}, {2, 3, 2, 0}, {0, 4, 5, 6},
                         {2, 8, 9, 7}};
        int[][][] temps = {site1, site2, site3, site4};
        Temperatures3D week = new Temperatures3D(temps);
        SiteDayAvg dayAvg;
        System.out.format("Average temp over all sites: %.3f%n",
                          week.avgTemp());

        for (int site = 1; site <= temps.length; site++)
        {
            dayAvg = week.siteMax(site);
            System.out.format("Hottest average day at site ");
            System.out.format("%d was day %d at %.3fC%n",
                              site, dayAvg.getDay(), dayAvg.getTemp())
        }
    }
}
```

Note that there aren't many changes from the 2D code, but overall the structure is much cleaner.

14.8 Exercises

General questions

1. If `quest1` is a 3D array of int values declared using

    ```
    int [][] quest1 = {{{1, 2}, {3, 4, 5}},
                       {{6}},
                       {{7, 8, 9, 10}, {11, 12}}};
    ```

    What is the value of `quest1[0][1][1]`? Which of the following are allowed, and for each valid one give its value: `quest1[1][1][1]`, `quest1[2][1][1]`, `quest1[1][0][0]`, `quest1[0][2][2]`.

174

2. For the array in Question 1, what will be output by the following `for` loop?

```
int sum = 0;
for (int i = 0; i < quest1.length; i++)
    sum += quest1[i][0][0];
System.out.println(sum);
```

3. For the array in Question 1, what will be output by the following nested `for` loop?

```
int sum = 0;
for (int i = 0; i < quest1.length; i++)
    for (int j = 0; j < quest1[i].length; j++)
        sum += quest1[i][j][0];
System.out.println(sum);
```

In-lab Programs

1. Write and test a method `public int[][] getMatrix()` which uses a Scanner object to input the number of rows and columns in a 2D rectangular array. Then read in the `int` values to populate the array, and return it from the method.

2. Create a class called `MatrixMult` that will have two instance fields, `matrixA` and `matrixB`, both of which are 2D arrays of doubles. The constructor will have two matrices as parameters, `in_matrixA` and `in_matrixB`, which will provide values to the two instance fields as usual. The method `public double[] getColumnOfB(int column)` will return a 1D array containing the values in the specified column of matrixB. Include the method `public double dotProduct(double[] vectorA, double[] vectorB)` returns the dot product of the two vectors, which is the sum of the products of all pairs of values from the two arrays. E.g., `dotProduct({3, 1, 0, 2, -1}, {2, 0, 1, 1, 2})` is 3 * 2 + 1 * 0 + 0 * 1 + 2 * 1 + -1 * 2, which is 6. The method `public void printMatrix()` outputs a 2D array of doubles, with each row on a new line and each column lined up. Output elements using `%6.2f`, as no values will be as big as `1000.0`.

Out-lab Programs

1. Write and test a class called `Methods2D` that has no instance fields or constructor but has four methods: `public static int max2D(int[][] myArray)` returns the largest value in the array, `public static int second2D(int[][] myArray)` returns the second largest element, `public static double average2D(int[][] myArray)` returns the average of the

175

array values, and `public static boolean isRect2D(int[][] myArray)` determines whether or not the array is rectangular.

2. Write and test a class called `Methods3D` that has no instance fields or constructor but has three methods: `public static int max3D(int[][][] myArray)` returns the largest value in the array, `public static int second3D(int[][][] myArray)` returns the second largest element, and `public static double average3D(int[][][] myArray)` returns the average of the array values.

3. Change `dotProduct()` and `getColumn()` in in-lab 3 from `public` to `private`. They will be used internally to perform a matrix multiplication, and were only `public` initially so that it was easy to test them. Add a method `private boolean legalMult()` which determines whether the matrices `matrixA` and `matrixB` can be multiplied. This means that (a) both matrices are rectangular and (b) the number of columns in `matrixA` is equal to the number of rows in `matrixB`. Write a method `public double[][] multiply()` which returns the matrix product of `matrixA` and `matrixB`. If `matrixA` is m x n and `matrixB` is n x p then the result is an m x p matrix where the `[i][j]` element is the dot product of row i of `matrixA` and row j of `matrixB`. Use the methods from the in-lab and this program to do the calculation.

Chapter 15. Recursive Methods

15.1 Introduction

Recursion is a powerful programming technique that you should become comfortable with because there are many situations where using it will greatly simplify programming tasks. A recursive method is one that calls on itself as it runs. This sounds a bit weird, so I'll start by looking at the traditional first example, computing factorials.

15.2 A Recursive Example: Computing Factorials

Consider computing the factorial of some non-negative integer value *n*. We know that it is usually written as *n*! and that its value is 1 * 2 * ... * *n*. Mathematicians define this more formally by saying that *n*! is 1 if *n* = 1, and is *n* * (*n* – 1)! otherwise. More commonly they also handle zero, which gives the definition that *n*! is 1 if *n* = 0, and is *n* * (*n* – 1)! otherwise.

How do we program this? One way is to use a loop and say:

```
public static int factorial(int n)
{
    int fact = 1;
    for (int i = 1; i <= n; i++)
        fact *= i;
    return fact;
}
```

This is called the iterative or non-recursive solution. Another way is to follow the mathematical definition and use the definition of the `factorial()` method within itself. This very directly leads to:

```
public static int factorial(int n)
{
    if (n == 0)
        return 1;
    else
        return n * factorial(n - 1);
}
```

This is called a recursive method because `factorial()` is called inside `factorial()`. Essentially the code has two parts, the base part that handles the simplest case (in this method when *n* is zero) and the recursive part that handles a more complex case by relying on recursion to give us the value of a simpler case. So if you are computing 6!, for example, the recursive part says "get me the value of 5! (which is

120), and multiply that by 6 to give me 6! (which will be 720)."

So the obvious question will be how does it know how to get the value of 5!? The best answer is to say "who cares?" and just to treat recursion as magic and use it without question. This is how you'll learn to think when programming recursively. However, if this offends you, this time I'll look at what is actually happening.

When I called `factorial(6)` it said to return `6 * factorial(5)`. So it calls `factorial(5)` which, since `5 != 0`, is computed as `5 * factorial(4)`. Similarly `factorial(4)` is `4 * factorial(3)`, `factorial(3)` is `3 * factorial(2)`, `factorial(2)` is `2 * factorial(1)`, and `factorial(1)` is `1 * factorial(0)`, and finally `factorial(0)` uses the base part, which says that if `(n == 0)` return 1, so it is 1. Feeding this back into all of the calculations that are hanging and waiting for results this tells us that `factorial(1)` is `1 * 1` which is 1, `factorial(2)` is `2 * 1` which is 2, `factorial(3)` is `3 * 2` which is 6, `factorial(4)` is `4 * 6` which is 24, `factorial(5)` is `5 * 24` which is 120, and finally `factorial(6)` is `6 * 120` which is 720, as expected.

The last paragraph is awful and the trick is to never think of recursive methods in this way, but to always use the trust in magic approach. This says that as long as you handle the simplest case first in the base part and then in the recursive part only rely on simpler cases than the one that you are currently handling, then your recursive method will always work. This can be proven using a mathematical method called proof by induction, but you shouldn't care about that but should just rely on it always working. That is, believe in magic.

In the case of a method to compute factorial there is no gain in using a recursive method and compared to the iterative method, so now I'll look at a problem where the recursive solution is trivial but the non-recursive method is much messier.

15.3 Tower of Hanoi: A Recursive Solution

There is an ancient fable (possibly created in 1883 by François Édouard Anatole Lucas) that says that there is a monastery in Hanoi (or in India in many versions) where the monks are solving a problem. They have three big pegs and originally 64 golden disks were placed on one of the pegs. The disks all have different sizes so they were stacked in the order of their size, with the smallest on top and the largest on the bottom. The monks' goal is to move all of the disks from the first peg to the third peg. There are, however, two rules. They can only move one disk at a time, and a larger disk can never be placed on top of a smaller disk. Once they have completed this task by legally moving all 64 disks across, the world will end.[38]

Assume that you are given the job of writing a program that will tell them the correct moves to take so that the world will end as fast as possible. How will you write this?

What you should do first is to look at some simpler cases. Say that the pegs are numbered 1, 2, and 3, and that you want to move three disks from peg 1 to peg 3. The way to do this is to get the top two disks from peg 1 to peg 2 using legal moves, move the biggest disk from peg 1 to peg 3, and then move the two smallest disks that are currently on peg 2 to peg 3. So this leaves two subtasks: how do you move two small disks from peg 1 to peg 2, and how do you move two small disks from peg 2 to peg 3. To do the first one, first move the smallest from peg 1 to peg 3, then the second smallest from peg 1 to peg 2, and then the smallest one back from peg 3 to peg 2. There is a similar solution to the second subtask. Putting this all together the instructions to follow are:

```
1 ⇒ 3
1 ⇒ 2
3 ⇒ 2
1 ⇒ 3
2 ⇒ 1
2 ⇒ 3
1 ⇒ 3
```

where $a \Rightarrow b$ means move the highest disk from peg a to peg b.

We need to debug our program on smaller examples like this because with 64 disks there will be 18,446,744,073,709,551,615 of these moves if we get everything right.

So now that I know what I'm doing, how do I write the program? I'll look at a recursive solution. If you aren't convinced that recursion is useful, go ahead and work on the iterative solution, which will be much harder. I'll first have a `Hanoi` class, which has one method called `makeMoves()` that makes the moves and three instance fields, *n*, *pegA* and *pegB*, where I want to move *n* disks from *pegA* to *pegB*. A typical instance of the class will be

```
Hanoi priests = new Hanoi(64, 1, 3);
```

so that `priests.makeMoves()` will give the priests their instructions on how to move the disks correctly starting at peg 1 and ending at peg 3. The only question is how to write this method. I'm going to do this recursively so I need to decide on the

---

[38] This is a very optimistic estimate for the world's end. Some of these disks must be pretty large, so if we assume that it takes 10 seconds on average to move a disk from one peg to another, that they never take a break, and that they never make a mistake (i.e., they always do the best moves), then the world will end in about 5,845,540,492,538 years, six months, and 20 days from when they started.

simplest case, which is when I only have one disk, in which case I just want to print out the instruction *pegA ==> pegB*. So my code will have the form:

```
if (n == 1)
    System.out.format("%d ==> %d%n", pegA, pegB);
else
{
    // handle the complicated case
}
```

Now I want to program the complicated case to move *n* (where *n* > 1) disks from *pegA* to *pegB*. Let's call the other peg *otherPeg*. What I need to do is to move the top (*n* – 1) disks from *pegA* to *otherPeg*, move the bottom disk from *pegA* to *pegB*, and then move the (*n* – 1) disks (that I put out of the way on *otherPeg*) from *otherPeg* to *pegB*. So the code is just:

```
Hanoi firstmove = new Hanoi(n - 1, pegA, otherPeg);
firstmove.makeMoves();

System.out.format("%d ==> %d%n", pegA, pegB);

Hanoi secondmove = new Hanoi(n - 1, otherPeg, pegB);
secondmove.makeMoves();
```

I can now complete the class. A minor detail is that *pegA*, *pegB*, and *otherPeg* are, in some order, the numbers 1, 2, and 3, so their sum is always 6. So I can compute *otherPeg* as shown in the class definition, below:

```
public class Hanoi
{
    // instance fields
    private int n;
    private int pegA;
    private int pegB;

    // Constructor for objects of class TestitClass
    public Hanoi(int in_n, int in_pegA, int in_pegB)
    {
        n = in_n;
        pegA = in_pegA;
        pegB = in_pegB;
    }

    // output the correct moves
    public void makeMoves()
    {
        if (n == 1)
            System.out.format("%d ==> %d%n", pegA, pegB);
        else
        {
            int otherPeg = 6 - pegA - pegB;   // 1 + 2 + 3 = 6
            Hanoi firstmove = new Hanoi(n - 1, pegA, otherPeg);
            firstmove.makeMoves();
            System.out.format("%d ==> %d%n", pegA, pegB);
            Hanoi secondmove = new Hanoi(n - 1, otherPeg, pegB);
            secondmove.makeMoves();
        }
    }
}
```

Note that the code does exactly what I said that we should do; move ($n - 1$) pegs out of the way onto the other peg, move the last one across, and then move the ($n - 1$) to their target destination. Testing this with

```
Hanoi fiveMoves = new Hanoi(5, 1, 3);
fiveMoves.makeMoves();
```

this gives the optimal list of 31 moves (moving n disks takes $2^n - 1$ moves)::

```
1 ==> 3
1 ==> 2
3 ==> 2
1 ==> 3
2 ==> 1
2 ==> 3
1 ==> 3
1 ==> 2
3 ==> 2
3 ==> 1
2 ==> 1
3 ==> 2
1 ==> 3
1 ==> 2
3 ==> 2
1 ==> 3
2 ==> 1
2 ==> 3
1 ==> 3
2 ==> 1
3 ==> 2
3 ==> 1
2 ==> 1
2 ==> 3
1 ==> 3
1 ==> 2
3 ==> 2
1 ==> 3
2 ==> 1
2 ==> 3
1 ==> 3
```

In this program I have taken the approach of creating Hanoi objects and calling the makeMoves() methods on them. This was mainly so that I could show that I can create objects of a class within the class definition. A more common solution to this problem would be to just create a static void method that directly output the moves. This would give the following, where I have also included a method that checks for valid input before calling on the recursive method.

```
public static void hanoiMoves(int n, int pegA, int pegB)
{
    if (n < 1 || pegA < 1 || pegA > 3 || pegB < 1 || pegB > 3)
        System.out.format("Illegal values, n: %d, pegs: %d, %d%n",
                          n, pegA, pegB);
    else
        legalHanoi(n, pegA, pegB);
}
// continued on next page
```

```
public static void legalHanoi(int n, int pegA, int pegB)
{
    if (n == 1)
        System.out.format("%d ==> %d%n", pegA, pegB);
    else
    {
        int otherPeg = 6 - pegA - pegB;
        legalHanoi(n - 1, pegA, otherPeg);
        System.out.format("%d ==> %d%n", pegA, pegB);
        legalHanoi(n - 1, otherPeg, pegB);
    }
}
```

15.4 Rules for Defining A Recursive Method

As these examples have shown, a recursive method has two parts, the base part and the recursive call part. So any recursive program should have a structure that follows:

```
if (base condition)
    // handle the base case
else
    // make recursive call(s)
```

The base case is the simplest case. For factorial this was when *n* was zero, and for Tower of Hanoi it was moving a single disk. Once you have decided on the simplest cases it is usually trivial to write the code to handle it.

The recursive code is, in most cases, fairly simple. The rule is that as long as it only relies on recursive calls that are simpler than the current call, then everything will work correctly. Simpler means that they will eventually lead to the simplest case that was your base case.

15.5 Recursive Loops

The place where recursion can go wrong is if the simplest case is never reached, which gives rise to a recursive loop. For example, look at my original code for the factorial() method:

```
public static int factorial(int n)
{
    if (n == 0)
        return 1;
    else
        return n * factorial(n - 1);
}
```

and think about what will happen if I try to evaluate factorial(-5). It will call on factorial(-6), which will call on factorial(-7), and so on. After a while Java will throw an error condition called a StackOverflowError, and will terminate. If you see this error, it almost always means that you have a recursive loop. To avoid this, your code should always handle not only "normal" inputs but also should handle incorrect cases. In this case the easiest approach would be to have two methods, first factorial() which just checs to make sure that the input is valid, and then another method, which it calls for valid data to calculate the factorial, which is the same approach that I used for hanoiMoves(), above. For example,

```java
public static int factorial(int n)
{
    if (n < 0)
    {
        System.out.format("Invalid input: %d%n", n);
        return -1;
    }
    else
        return factGood(n);
}

public static int factGood(int n)
{
    if (n == 0)
        return 1;
    else
        return n * factGood(n - 1);
}
```

A better approach is to raise a user-defined exception if invalid data is attempted, and I'll be describing that approach in Chapter 18.

As another example of a recursive loop, consider the following code to find the product $n * (n - 3) * (n - 6) * ... * 1$.

```java
public static int product(int n)
{
    if (n == 1)
        return 1;
    else
        return n * product(n - 3);
}
```

If *n* is 7 this will return 7 * 4 * 1, which is 28. However, if you try, say, a value of 8 for *n*, it will attempt to multiply 8 * 5 * 2 * -1 * -4 ... and Java will, after a short time, throw a StackOverflowError to show a recursive loop.

15.6 Why Recursion Is Importantant to Programmers

Recursion is particularly important when you get into more advanced data structures like trees. For example say that you have a list of numbers and that numbers keep getting added to the list and removed from the list. We want to be able to quickly find out if a particular number is in the list. One way to do this is with a binary search tree that could look like, for example,

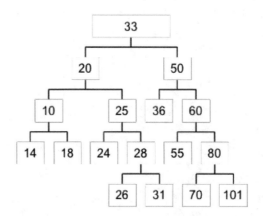

The property of these trees is that anything that is in the left subtree of a node (at any level in the tree) is less than the value of the node, and any value in the right subtree is greater than the node's value. Now say we want to know whether a value is in the tree. Start at the root node. Compare the search value against this node value, if the values are equal you are done. If they are not equal and the current node is a leaf, then the value isn't in the tree. Otherwise if the value is less than the current node value, then recursively call the search on the left subtree and if it is greater recursively call the search on the right subtree.

For example, if we want to know whether 28 is in the tree, we'll compare it to 33, move left, compare it to 20, move right, compare it to 25, move right, compare it to 28, and announce that it is in the tree. If we want to know whether 57 is in the tree, the comparisons wil be against 33, 50, 60, and 55, and since we've reached a leaf, we'll announce that it isn't in the tree.

So recursively most tree algorithms, including this one, are trivial, but iteratively most are a mess.

15.7 Recursively Analyzing an Array

In this section I'll look at a simple example of working through a 1D array to find its largest value. Previously you have seen how to do this with a for loop, and so now I'll use recursion.

I'll look at a more general problem here - how to find the biggest value between indices min and max of the array, where min is less than or equal to max. To then find the biggest value in the whole array I just need to set min to 0 and max to the array's

184

largest index.

The basic idea of the program is that if we are just looking at a range with one element (i.e., min == max) then we want to return that value. Otherwise return the largest of the first value and the biggest value in the rest of the array, which is a recursive definition.

I'll put my recursive max() method into a class called Recursive whose constructor's only parameter is a 1D array of integers. The constructor will just pass in a value for this array, so isn't very interesting.

The method header will be

```
public int maxRange(int min, int max)
```

which will implement the recursive design described above. It begins with a validity check on the values on min and max and then gets into the important code where first it checks for the base case (min == max), and then compares the first element in the range against a recursive call to find the largest value in the rest of the array.

The code is shown below:

```
public class Recursive
{
    // instance fields
    private int[] intArray;

    // Constructor for objects of class Recursive
    public Recursive(int[] in_intArray)
    {
        intArray = in_intArray;
    }

    // recursively find the largest value in the array from indices
    // min to max
    public int maxRange(int min, int max)
    {
        if (min > max || min < 0 || max >= intArray.length)
        {
            System.out.format("Invalid range: %d, %d%n", min, max);
            return -1;
        }

        if (min == max)
            return intArray[min];
        else
        {
            int bigRest = maxRange(min + 1, max);
            if (intArray[min] > bigRest)
                return intArray[min];
            else
                return bigRest;
        }
    }
}
```

The thing to look at here is the short chunk of code that begins with
`if (min == max)` which is the critical definition. It begins with the base case where there is only one element, and returns it, then follows this with the recursive call. Play with the code to make sure that you understand what is going on. If you have concerns, and most will at first, copy the code into BlueJ and run it under the debugger so that you can watch the changing values.

In the method `maxRange()` I needed the parameters min and max so that I could do the recursive call. In general, however, I'll want a method called, say maxVector() which returns the maximum value in the complete vector. To do this just add this method as:

```
public int maxVector()
{
    return maxRange(0, intArray.length - 1;
}
```

and this becomes the method that users will use to find the largest value in an array. The method `maxRange()` is now just an internel method that users don't need to know about, so it should be changed to `private`.

To test the code I used the following:

```
public class RecursiveTest extends junit.framework.TestCase
{
    public void testRecursive()
    {
        int[] testArray = {7, 18, -5, -17, 93, 14, 6, 8};
        Recursive arrayObject = new Recursive(testArray);
        assertEquals(arrayObject.maxVector(), 93);
    }
}
```

15.8 Exercises

General questions

1. The body of the `makeMoves()` method for Tower of Hanoi began:

    ```
    if (n == 1)
        System.out.format("%d ==> %d%n", pegA, pegB);
    ```

    How, if at all, would the results have been different if these two lines had been replaced with:

    ```
    if (n == 0);
        // do nothing
    ```

and no other changes were made to the method? Explain.

2. Consider the following recursive method:

```
public static int quest2(int n)
{
    if (n == 0 || n == 1)
        return n;
    else
        return 2 * n + quest2(n - 3);
}
```

What will be the values of quest2(9), quest2(8), and quest2(7)?

3. Consider the following recursive method:

```
public static void quest3(int x, double y)
{
    if (x == 0)
        return y;
    else
        return x * quest3(x - 1, y - 1):
}
```

What is the value of quest3(4, 2)?

4. In the method maxRange() I had two parameters, min and max. What changes would I have to make to just have a single parameter, min, where the method returns the largest value between min and the end of the array? Which would be the better approach for this problem?

5. Fibonacci numbers are defined by fibonacci(1) = fibonacci(2) = 1, and fibonacci(n) = fibonacci(n – 1) + fibonacci(n – 2)

In-lab programs

1. Modify the maxRange() method as described in Question 4, above.

2. Add two methods called min() and minRange() to the Recursive class, similar to max() and maxRange(), that return the smallest value in the array.

3. Add a class called TwoInts which has two int instance fields named int1 and int2, a constructor to set them, and two public methods getInt1() and getInt2() to return their values. Then modify minRange() so that it returns a TwoInts pair which contain the smallest value in the array and the index at which it is located.

4. Create a new class Recursive2D, which uses recursive methods to find the largest value in a 2D array, which is the only instance field.

Out-lab programs

1. Add a method sort() to the Recursive class that sorts the elements of the array, which means that the elements of the array are rearranged so that the array contains the same values but in increasing order. It will need a recursive method sortRange(int min, int max). There are a number of ways to do this; use a strategy in the recursive step where you use minRange() from Question 3, above, to find the smallest value in the rest of the array and its location, exchange it with the first element in the array if it is smaller, and then sort the rest. This is a somewhat inefficient approach to sorting an array, but the point is to get used to recursion.

2. If you are offended by the inefficient approach taken in question 1, above, add a method quickSort() to sort the array. Google quicksort to find details on the algorithm. Obviously if you find code for quicksort, don't copy it.

3. Another efficient solution would be to use a merge sort. Again use a search engine to find the definition of this sort.

4. Include a counter of the number of comparisons made in your quicksort or merge sort and in the original sort from out-lab Question 1. Sort random arrays of different lengths (E.g., 100, 500, 1000, and 2000 elements) and plot the number of comparisons made by each sort. Math.random() can be used in a loop to generate random values in a vector. Can you speculate of the growth patterns for the two sorting techniques?

5. Fibonacci numbers are defined by fibonacci(1) = fibonacci(2) = 1, and fibonacci(n) = fibonacci(n – 1) + fibonacci(n – 2) for n > 2, giving the sequence 1, 1, 2, 3, 5, 8, 13, 21, 34, ... Write a recursive method called fibonacci() that directly implements this definition. Test your method by calculating fibonacci(20). Inside the code count how many different times fibonacci(10) is recalculated. What has gone wrong here and what does this tell you about times where recursion should be avoided? How should you write this method.

Chapter 16. Inheritance

16.1 Introduction

One of the most powerful features of Object-Oriented Design and Object-Oriented Programming is called *inheritance*, which I'll be describing in this chapter. I'll mainly use an example program to describe it, with a lot of commentary as I go.

Later in this chapter I'll discuss cohesiveness, which is the concept that classes are expected to contain very similar fields and methods that can be applied to these fields. As an example of a class that wouldn't be cohesive consider a `TransportDevice` class that contained definitions for cars, planes, ships, and possibly space shuttles, where many of the methods would only apply to some of the devices. For example, docking makes sense, in very different ways, for ships and space shuttles, but not for cars and planes. So it is better to have different classes for individual devices and include methods in those classes that are appropriate for them. The problem with this is that some methods (e.g., scheduling) might be appropriate for many or all of the devices, and so there is a danger that we might have to duplicate these methods in each class. Inheritance gets around this problem, and as it does this, it also creates a wonderful hierarchical class design system.

In the case described above inheritance lets us define a `TransportDevice` class that contains field and methods that are common to all of the devices, and then create subclasses called `Car`, `Ship`, etc., that describe these objects and methods that are specific to these objects. We'll have access to the methods in the `TransportDevice` class, and can either use them or replace them with new versions in subclasses. Then once we've done this, we might decide that a `Porsche` is different from a `Chevy`, and make subclasses of the `Car` class with name like `Chevy`, `Porsche`, and `Lamborghini`. Or maybe I'll break `Car` into two subclasses, `Foreign` and `Domestic`, and then break them down into deeper subclasses. These classes will be sharing or redefining and adding methods as we work down through the class inheritance tree.

16.2 An Inheritance Example

I'll be using this example throughout this chapter because it introduces all of the important features of inheritance.

The problem will be to analyze three kinds of people, professors, students, and office staff. All of these people share the fact that they are people and so will have some things in common. If, for example, ithey are aged 19, they will be described as a teenager, if they are 72 or older, they can ski free at Bridger Bowl in Bozeman, MT, and so on. But there are also many ways in which they are very different. For example, a student will be discouraged if they have more than four years left before they expect to graduate or if their expectation of when they will get a real job is further away than their expected graduation. Faculty will be much happier if they have tenure. Office staff will be much happier if they work in the CS office, and so on.

This leads to deciding that I need four classes, a *superclass* called `Person` and three *subclasses* called `Student`, `Faculty`, and `OfficeStaff`. The superclass will contain fields and methods that are usually applicable to objects in each subclass. The subclasses will have additional fields, additional methods that are specialized for these objects, and in some cases methods that replace the superclass methods when they aren't applicable.

The `Person` class will have four instance fields, `String name`, `int age`, `boolean employed`, and `double income`, which have the obvious meanings. The `boolean` field `employed` will be true if the person is currently employed. It will have two methods, `int happiness()` that will estimate how happy the person is based on the values of the fields, and `String describeAge()`, which will describe them based on their age (e.g., it their age is 16, they will be described as a teen).

The `Professor` class will be a subclass to the `Person` class. It will have two new fields, `String rank` (e.g., "`Associate Professor`"), and `boolean tenured`, which specifies whether or not they have been awarded tenure. It will also have access to fields that are in the `Person` class, which is its superclass. Happiness is described differently for professors than for many other people, since it largely depends on whether they are tenured. So the `Professor` class will have its own `happiness()` method. On the other hand, their age description will be the same as for anyone else, and so it will use the `describeAge()` method from its parent class, `Person`.

The `Student` class will have two new fields, `int yearsToGrad` and `int yearsToRealJob`, which will be estimates of how many years it will take the student to get their degree and how many years it will be until they get a new job. `Student` will use the `describeAge()` and `happiness()` methods from its superclass, `Parent`, but will also have a new method, just applicable to students, called `boolean discouraged()` that checks to see whether the student should be discouraged, which will be true if they are more than four years from graduation, if they are not expecting to get a real job when they graduate, or if they are older than 40 and are still a student.

The officeStaff class will have one new field, String dept, which gives the department where they work. It will also have replacement methods for both happiness() and describeAge() because obviously they will be happiest if they are working for Computer Science and they are always young.

Now I just need to implement all this, and use that to show how inheritance works in Java.

16.2.1 The Person superclass

This will be a normal class that we should be familiar with by now. You don't tell Java that a class is a superclass, but when we create the three subclasses, we'll tell Java that they are subclasses to this class.

```java
public class Person
{
    // instance fields
    private String name;
    private int age;
    private boolean employed;
    private double income;

    // Constructor for objects of class Person
    public Person(String in_name, int in_age, boolean in_employed,
                  double in_income)
    {
        name = in_name;
        age = in_age;
        employed = in_employed;
        income = in_income;
    }

    public int happiness()
    {
        int happy;
        if (employed)
        {
            happy = (int) income / 10000;
            if (happy > 10)
                happy = 10;
        }
        else if (age < 30)
            happy = 5;
        else happy = 2;

        return happy;
    }
// continued on next page
```

```
    public String describeAge()
    {
        if (age < 2)
            return "baby";
        else if (age < 13)
            return "child";
        else if (age < 20)
            return "teen";
        else if (age < 72)
            return "adult";
        else
            return "free skier at Bridger Bowl";
    }

    public String getName()
    {
        return name;
    }

    public int getAge()
    {
        return age;
    }
}
```

16.2.2 The Sudent subclass

I'll give the code first, and then comment on in it in considerable detail.

```
public class Student extends Person
{
    // instance fields
    private int yearsToGrad,
                yearsToRealJob;

    // Constructor for objects of class Student
    public Student(String in_name, int in_age, boolean in_employed,
                   double in_income, int in_yearsToGrad,
                   int in_yearsToRealJob)
    {
        // the next line must be the first line in Student's
        // constructor
        super(in_name, in_age, in_employed, in_income);
        yearsToGrad = in_yearsToGrad;
        yearsToRealJob = in_yearsToRealJob;
    }

    public boolean discouraged()
    {
        return (yearsToGrad > 4 || yearsToRealJob > yearsToGrad
                    || getAge() > 40);
    }
}
```

The header line for the class now includes extends Person. This is the way that Java specifies that this class is a subclass of the Person class, which becomes its superclass.

The constructor for Student has six entries, the four for Person plus two more that are specific to Student objects. So a typical Student declaration would be:

192

```
Student jim = new Student("James Peters", 24, false, 500, 3, 8);
```

which would say that his full name is James Peters, he is 24, he is unemployed, his income is $500, he expects to graduate in three years, and he doesn't expect to get a real job for eight years.

The first line of the constructor code is

```
super(inname, inage, inemployed, inincome);
```

This will call the superclass's constructor to save values in that class's instance fields. There are two important things to note here. (a) This call to the parent's constructor must be the first line of the child's constructor. If you place it in a later line,, there will be an error. (b) To call the parent's constructor we always use super(params) and cannot say, in our current example, Person(params).

Note that although I'll want to apply the methods happiness() and describeAge() to objects from the class Student, I haven't mentioned them in class Student's code. If, after defining jim as shown above, I want to find the value of jim.happiness(), I can do that directly. Effectively what will happen is that Java will know that jim has type Student, and will look for the method happiness() in class Student's code. When it doesn't find it there, it will look in the superclass's code, find happiness() there, and use that definition. So a method in a superclass is available to an object, unless it is redefined in the subclass code.

As I show here I can also declare a new method, discouraged(), in this code. It can only be used on instances of the Student class.

discouraged() needs to know the student's age so that it can check to see whether they are over 40. Since age is a private field in the parent class, one has to use a method, in this case getAge() to get the student's age from Person.

16.2.3 The Professor subclass

The code for this class is shown on the next page.

```
public class Professor extends Person
{
    // instance fields
    private String rank;
    private boolean tenured;

    // Constructor for objects of class Professor
    public Professor(String in_name, int in_age, double in_income,
                     String in_rank, boolean in_tenured)
    {
        super(in_name, in_age, true, in_income);

        rank = in_rank;
        tenured = in_tenured;
    }

    public int happiness()
    {
        if (tenured)
        {
            if (rank.equals("Professor"))
                return 10;
            else if (rank.equals("Associate Professor"))
                return 9;
            else
                return 8;
        } else
            return 10 - getAge() / 10; // I'm assuming that there are no
                                       // untenured faculty aged >= 110
    }
}
```

As discussed earlier, I have two new instance fields, String rank and boolean tenured.

A Professor object is created with a call like:

```
Professor joan = new Professor("Joan Smith", 40, 45000,
                               "Associate Professor", true);
```

Which says that Joan Smith is 40, makes $45,000 as an Associate Professor, and is tenured. Note that there is no mention of whether or not she is employed. I'm assuming that anyone who calls themselves a professor is employed, so in the class definition true is put into the constructor call for the parent class to say that this object is employed.

In this class I've redefined the happiness() method by providing a new method definition. If happiness() is called on an instance of Professor, this is the definition that will be used.

16.2.4 The OfficeStaff subclass

The code for this class is shown on the next page:

194

```
public class OfficeStaff extends Person
{
    // instance fields
    private String dept;

    // Constructor for objects of class OfficeStaff
    public OfficeStaff(String in_name, double in_income,
                       String in_dept)
    {
        super(in_name, 29, true, in_income);
        dept = in_dept;
    }

    public int happiness()
    {
        if (dept.equals("CS"))
            return 10;
        else return 8;
    }

    public String describeAge()
    {
        return("always young");
    }
}
```

There is just one new field here, dept. The constructor just has three parameters, so a typical call will be

```
OfficeStaff adam = new OfficeStaff("Adam Smith", 25000, "ECE");
```

Two of the Person fields, age and employed, have not been included because office staff always appear to be 29 and obviously they are employed. So in the super constructor call to Person I've had to include those values.

In this class I've redefined both happiness() and describeAge(), since the definitions in the parent class weren't appropriate for office staff.

16.2.5 Class diagram for the inheritance example

Inheritance is shown with an arrow with an open triangular head from the subclass to the class that it extends, as shown in the BlueJ diagram on the top of the next page.

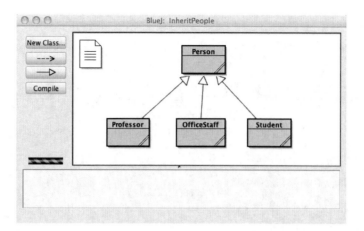

16.2.6 UnitTest class for the inheritance example

The following unit test gives examples of objects in all four classes (Professor, Student, OfficeStaff, and Person) and shows how the methods behave for each one.

```java
public class UnitTest
{
    public static void main()
    {
        Professor fred = new Professor("Fred Smith", 55, 60000,
                                       "Professor", true);
        System.out.format("Fred's happiness: %d%n", fred.happiness());
        System.out.format("Fred's age class: %s%n%n",fred.describeAge());

        OfficeStaff janice = new OfficeStaff("Janice Roberts", 35000,
                                             "CS");
        System.out.format("Janice's happiness: %d%n", janice.happiness());
        System.out.format("Janice's age class: %s%n%n",
                          janice.describeAge());

        Student tom = new Student("Tom Jones", 20, false, 0, 4, 6);
        System.out.format("Tom's happiness: %d%n", tom.happiness());
        System.out.format("Toms's age class: %s%n", tom.describeAge());
        if (tom.discouraged())
            System.out.format("Tom is discouraged%n%n");
        else
            System.out.format("Tom is not discouraged%n");

        Person peter = new Person("Peter Scott", 75, false, 70000);
        System.out.format("Peter's happiness: %d%n", peter.happiness());
        System.out.format("Peter's age class: %s%n%n",
                          peter.describeAge());
    }
}
```

which gives the following output:

```
Fred's happiness: 10
Fred's age class: adult

Janice's happiness: 10
Janice's age class: always young

Tom's happiness: 5
Toms's age class: adult
Tom is discouraged

Peter's happiness: 2
Peter's age class: free skier at Bridger
```

16.3 Cohesion

The concept of cohesion is related to inheritance. When you design a class, it should be *cohesive*. This means that it should represent a single kind of thing and the methods that operate on those kinds of things. If, for example, you have a class called `TransportMachine`, then it might have objects that are cars, and other objects that are boats, and so on. Then some of the methods will apply to cars but not boats, others to planes but not to cars, and so on. This would be poor cohesion, and it would be better to have a class for cars with their methods, a class for boats with their methods, and then use inheritance to keep common methods in a parent class.

16.4 Summary

In this example I have shown all of the important features of inheritance. The `Person` class was a parent or superclass to the three subclasses, `Professor`, `Student`, and `OfficeStaff`.

Some of the important features are:

To specify that new class A is a subclass of class B use the header:

```
public class A extends B
```

In the constructor for A the first line will be a call to one of B's constructors using

```
super(params)
```

If a method is applied to a class instance (i.e., an object), Java will first look in that class for a definition of the method, and will use that if it finds it. If not, it will look in the parent of the class, and so on up the inheritance tree until either it finds and uses a definition or it never finds it and has to tell the user that the method doesn't exist.

Subclasses cannot directly access instance fields in their superclasses, but must use methods to access them.

Inheritance trees can be arbitrarily deep. In my example I only had two levels of classes, but I could have, for example, made three subclasses of the `Student` class called `Undergrad`, `Grad`, and `Perpetual`, which would have increased the level by one. These three new classes would have access to everything above them including the methods `happiness()` and `describeAge()` from `Person` and `discouraged()` from `Student`.

Most Java programmers don't care, but all of the classes that you write are by default a subclass of a global class called `Object` unless they are placed lower in the tree by specifying that they extend another class. So if I wanted to, I could add `extends Object` to the header of every class that I write that doesn't extend another class, and it would make no difference. The reason that this does matter, even though most people don't care, is that `Object` includes a few useful methods that are available throughout the class tree. The two most valuable are `toString()`, which makes a `String` representation of any object, and `clone()`, which makes a copy of any object. Normally if you say

```
SomeClass fred = new SomeClass(params);
jane = fred;
```

then any changes to `jane` will also change `fred` because they are referencing the same object, but if instead you use:

```
jane = fred.clone();
```

then they will reference different objects and changes to one will not affect the other.

Inheritance tree structures can be arbitrarily deep. For example, I could create two new classes called `Undergrad` and `Grad`, which both extend the `Student` class. Clearly their `discouraged()` methods would be different. In this case `Person` and `Student` would both be superclases to the new classes and `Person` would still be a superclass to `Student`. `Object` would be a superclass to all of them.

16.5 Exercises

General questions

1. Based on the example in this chapter, if I create a new object with

    ```
    Professor jack = new Professor("Jack Frost", 59, 40000,
                                   "Assistant Professor", false);
    ```

    what would be the values of `jack.happiness()` and `jack.describeAge()`?

2. Explain how using inheritace can improve programming efficiency and program readability.

3. If you look at the code for a class, can you tell if it is a superclass for another class?

4. Can a class be both a superclass for one class and a subclass for a different class?

5. Say that a class named Fred has the structure:

```
public class Fred extends Julia
{
    int jane;
    Julia newJulia;
    public Fred(int in_jane, double in_john)
    {
        jane = in_jane;
        newJulia = new Julia(in_john);
    }
    // Fred's methods
}
```

Is this legal? Explain.

6. Say that a class named Fred has the structure:

```
public class Fred extends Julia
{
    int jane;
    public Fred(int in_jane, double in_john)
    {
        jane = in_jane;
        super(in_john);
    }
    // Fred's methods
}
```

Is this legal? Explain.

7. Say that five classes, A, B, C, D, and E, have the properties that A is a superclass, B and C both extend A, D extends C, and E extends D. Also assume that the methods w(), x(), y() and z() are defined as follows: w() is defined in C, x() is defined in A, B, and E, y() is defined in B and D, and z() is defined in D. Draw a chart which shows which methods can be used in each of the five classes, and where each of these calls is defined.

In-lab programs

1. Download Greenfoot from www.bluej.org, the same site from which you downloaded BlueJ at the beginning of the semester, and run the Wombat scenario.

2. Look through the Greenfoot code and change the size of the Greenfoot matrix.

3. Modify the Greenfoot code so that wherever the wombat changes direction you force it to turn the other way instead.

Out-lab programs

1. In the wombat scenario, the wombat heads to the side, turns, and then keeps going around the outside. Modify this so that on each move in the interior 80% of the time it heads ahead, as usual, 15% of the time it turns left, and 5% of the time it turns right. When it hits an edge half of the time it goes left and the other half it goes right. The method `Math.random()` could be useful.

2. Add seahorses and pizzas to the scenario, whose movement is the same as the modified wombat motion described in 1, above. Seahorses obviously eat pizza, but don't eat leaves, while wombats do the opposite. Create a new `Actor` extension called `Critter` so that you can use inheritance to put as much wombat and seahorse shared behavior as possible into `Critter`. The image files on Greenfoot include both seahorse and pizza images.

3. Create a superclass called `Vehicle` and three subclasses called `Shuttle`, `Helicopter`, and `Car`. `Vehicle` has one `String` field, name, and three `int` fields, avgSpeed, price, and mpg, all with the obvious meanings. It has two methods, `int tripTime(int distance)` and `int fuelUsed(int distance)`, also with obvious meanings. It has methods that return the values of each of its fields. `Shuttle` always assigns `Integer.MAX_VALUE` for price and 0 for mpg. It overrides the `fuelUsed()` method and returns `Integer.MAX_VALUE` from that method. It has an additional field, `int numMissions`, and a method `int missionsRemain()` which subtracts the current number of missions from 45. `Car` has a field `int seatbelts` and a method `boolean legal(passengers)` which determines whether there are sufficient seat belts for the number of passengers. `Helicopter` overrides the `tripTime(int distance)` method by adding three minutes for take off and three minutes for descent to the trip time computed by `distance / avgSpeed`. Create a good test suite to test all objects and methods.

200

Chapter 17. Interfaces, Polymorphism, and Packages

17.1 Introduction

As much as possible you want to reuse code that you have already implemented and tested. Java's interface structures often make this possible.

Say that I have a class named Analysis that performs statistical analyses of arrays of doubles with methods min() and max() that compute the minimum and maximum values in the array, and mean() that computes the mean (average) of all of the elements of the array, as shown below.

```java
public class Analysis
{
    public static double min(double[] numArray)
    {
        double minval = numArray[0];
        for (int i = 1; i < numArray.length; i++)
            if (numArray[i] < minval)
                minval = numArray[i];
        return minval;
    }

    public static double max(double[] numArray)
    {
        double maxval = numArray[0];
        for (int i = 1; i < numArray.length; i++)
            if (numArray[i] > maxval)
                maxval = numArray[i];
        return maxval;
    }

    public static double mean(double[] numArray)
    {
        double sum = 0;
        for (int i = 0; i < numArray.length; i++)
            sum += numArray[i];
        return sum / numArray.length;
    }
}
```

Now say that I want to do the same operations on my company records where each record, from a NameSalary class, contains a name and a salary, and I want to know the minimum, maximum, and mean salary in the company. I also want to do the same operations on my baseball team where each player's record, from a Player class, contains their name, team name, hits and at bats, and I want to be able to compute these statistics on player batting averages.

So what I'd like to be able to do is to use the min(), max(), and mean() methods from my Analysis class, which were expecting arrays of doubles, directly on my arrays of employee records and on arrays of player records. So a UnitTest class could be:

```
Player[] mariners = new Player[4];
// code not shown to get values into the mariners array

System.out.format("best batting average is %.3f%n",
                  Analysis.max(mariners));

System.out.format("worst batting average is %.3f%n",
                  Analysis.min(mariners));

System.out.format("average player batting average is %.3f%n",
                  Analysis.mean(mariners));

NameSalary[] myCompany = new NameSalary[3];
// code not shown to get values into the myCompany array

System.out.format("Minimum Salary is $%.0f%n",
                  Analysis.min(myCompany));

System.out.format("Maximum Salary is $%.0f%n",
                  Analysis.max(myCompany));

System.out.format("Mean Salary is $%.0f%n",
                  Analysis.mean(myCompany));
```

This is quite a leap forward because now my Analysis methods are also being directly applied to arrays of Player objects and arrays of NameSalary objects. What is happening is that the type of the object determines which method implementation is used, a process that is called *polymorphism*.

17.2 Using an Interface Class

Java lets me use this unit test by setting up an interface between the two classes (Player and NameSalary) and the values that I'm interested in for the Analysis class, which is expecting to deal with arrays of doubles. This interface will take the Player and NameSalary types and let them be viewed as a single named type, say called IAnalysis, and then requires that there is a way to extract the double values that the analysis routines need from the Player and NameSalary classes.

The mechanism that Java uses to do this is, conveniently, called an *interface*. For this application we'll call the interface IAnalysis. The code for this interface is very simple and is just:

```
public interface IAnalysis
{
    double getDouble();
}
```

This is saying that any class that implements this interface will be able to be accessed through the name IAnalysis, and that they must have a method called getDouble() that returns a double to be used by other classes. I'll look at the required structure in more detail later, but for now just see that the header contains the interface keyword and that it contains the header of the method that is required, under most circumstances, to be in all implementing classes.

Now let's look at the NameSalary class. It has to say that it goes through the IAnalysis and it must contain the method getDouble(),which will say how it wants to send out a double value.

Code for this is:

```
public class NameSalary implements IAnalysis
{
    // instance fields
    private String name;
    private int salary;

    // Constructor
    public NameSalary(String in_name, int in_salary)
    {
        name = in_name;
        salary = in_salary;
    }

    public int getSalary()
    {
        return salary;
    }

    // any other methods that the class needs

    public double getDouble()
    {
        return (double) salary;
    }
}
```

In the header line the keyword implements says that this class will go through the named interface, which in this case is IAnalysis.

NameSalary has two instance fields, String name and int salary. It will presumably have several methods, but I've only shown one apart from getDouble(), which is getSalary(), which returns an int. However, the interface requires that we have a getDouble() method that will return a double value through the interface. So this method just takes the salary field and returns it as a double.

The Player class needs to return the batting average through the getDouble() method. Its code will be:

```
public class Player implements IAnalysis
{
    // instance fields
    private String name;
    private String team;
    private int hits;
    private int atBats;

    // Constructor
    public Player(String in_name, String in_team, int in_hits,
                  int in_atBats)
    {
        name = in_name;
        team = in_team;
        hits = in_hits;
        atbats = in_atBats;
    }

    // any other methods that the class needs

    public double getDouble()
    {
        return (double) hits / atBats;
    }
}
```

Now I just need to modify the Analysis class code so that it will handle arrays of NameSalary and Player objects. The code to do this is shown below:

```
public class Analysis
{
    public static double min(IAnalysis[] numArray)
    {
        double minval = numArray[0].getDouble();
        for (int i = 1; i < numArray.length; i++)
            if (numArray[i].getDouble() < minval)
                minval = numArray[i].getDouble();
        return minval;
    }

    public static double max(IAnalysis[] numArray)
    {
        double maxval = numArray[0].getDouble();
        for (int i = 1; i < numArray.length; i++)
            if (numArray[i].getDouble() > maxval)
                maxval = numArray[i].getDouble();
        return maxval;
    }

    public static double mean(IAnalysis[] numArray)
    {
        double sum = 0;
        for (int i = 0; i < numArray.length; i++)
            sum += numArray[i].getDouble();
        return sum / numArray.length;
    }
}
```

To summarize what has happened here, we want the methods in Analysis to be able to work on arrays of different objects, even though its routines were designed for arrays of doubles. So instead I've set up an interface class called IAnalysis, and any object can pass double values through IAnalysis by using the getDouble()

204

method specified in the interface. Then `Analysis` is modified so that it operates on arrays of `IAnalysis`, and uses `getDouble()` to get the `double` values that it needs.

I'll just look at one method, `min()`. It returns a `double`, which is what we should expect. Its parameter is an array of type `IAnalysis`, which is the name of the interface. This will let us use an array of any type that implements the `IAnalysis` interface, and so in this case it lets us use arrays of either `Player` or `NameSalary` objects. It then needs to access the `double` components of these objects, which it does with the `getDouble()` method. Once one has this capability, the code is fairly direct. It starts `minval` with the value of the `double` part of the first array element, which is `numArray[0].getDouble()` and then compares `minval` against all of the other array values. Whenever it finds a smaller one, it updates `minval`, and finally returns the value of `minval`. Now I just need the unit test class:

```java
import java.util.*;  // needed for input Scanner
public class UnitTest
{
    public static void main()
    {
        String first, last,  // input names for a player
               name;         // combined name, first last.
        int hits, atBats;    // input player hits and at bats
        Scanner in = new Scanner(System.in);  // usual Scanner

        Player[] mariners = new Player[4];
        // read in player information. All players play for the
        // Mariners so that is set in the constructor
        for (int player = 0; player < mariners.length; player++)
        {
            System.out.println("Enter player's name (first last)");
            first = in.next();
            last = in.next();
            name = String.format("%s %s", first, last);
            System.out.format("Enter %s's hits and at bats
                               (two integers)%n", name);
            hits = in.nextInt();
            atBats = in.nextInt();
            mariners[player] = new Player(name, "Mariners", hits,
                                          atBats);
        }
        System.out.format("best batting average is %.3f%n",
                          Analysis.max(mariners));
        System.out.format("worst batting average is %.3f%n",
                          Analysis.min(mariners));
        System.out.format("average batting average is %.3f%n%n",
                          Analysis.mean(mariners));

        NameSalary[] myCompany = new NameSalary[3];
        myCompany[0] = new NameSalary("Denbigh", 50000);
        myCompany[1] = new NameSalary("Fred", 45000);
        myCompany[2] = new NameSalary("Jane", 60000);
        System.out.format("Minimum Salary is $%.0f%n",
                          Analysis.min(myCompany));
        System.out.format("Maximum Salary is $%.0f%n",
                          Analysis.max(myCompany));
        System.out.format("Mean Salary is $%.0f%n",
                          Analysis.mean(myCompany));
    }
}
```

which gives the session shown below, where **bold** shows user inputs.

```
Enter player's name (first last)
Edgar Martinez
Enter Edgar Martinez's hits and at bats (two integers)
300 700
Enter player's name (first last)
Steve Jones
Enter Steve Jones's hits and at bats (two integers)
1 101
Enter player's name (first last)
Peter Smith
Enter Peter Smith's hits and at bats (two integers)
30 125
Enter player's name (first last)
John Adams
Enter John Adams's hits and at bats (two integers)
20 205
best batting average is 0.429
worst batting average is 0.010
average batting average is 0.194

Minimum Salary is $40000
Maximum Salary is $60000
Mean Salary is $51667
```

A minor point is that the salary values were ints but I converted them to doubles for getDouble(). I've now printed them as ints in the output statements using a %.0f code. I could have cast to int and used %d but that would have given me an average salary of $51666 instead of the rounded $51667 that I got from using %.0f.

17.3 More Details on Interface and Implements Definitions

An interface definition will have the form:

```
public interface name
{
    constant declarations;
    abstract method declarations;
}
```

where the constant declarations, if present, must be static and final. These are fairly unusual, so I'll ignore them. By convention the name will begin with I.

An abstract method declaration can be thought of as just the header of a method, which means that you are defining the method interface (its name, its return type, and its parameters) without providing implementation code, since this will be provided by the method in the classes that implement the interface.

The header of a class that implements an interface will have the form:

```
accesstype class className extends Interface, Interface2, …
```

206

and so a class can implement more than one interface if needed. Usually the class will have method implementations for all of the methods in all of the listed interfaces.[39]

So if, for example, we have three interface definitions

```
public interface Inter1
{
    void output();
    int something(int x);
}

public interface Inter2
{
    double other()
}

public interface Inter3
{
    int fourth();
}
```

and a class named NewClass has the header

```
public class NewClass implements Inter1, Inter2
{
    // body of newclass
}
```

then the body of NewClass must contain full definitions for the output(), something(), and other() methods.

C programmers should note that the abstract class definitions (i.e., method headers) in the interface definitions are different from C function prototypes in that they include the name of any parameter, not just the type.

17.4 Packages

In many of your programs you've had to import packages like java.lang.String or javax.swing.event.[40] Since these have obviously been added during the development of new versions of Java, there must be a way for users to build these packages. Not only is this true, but in fact every time you write a Java program if you don't specify a package your classes will be added to a default package during its execution.

---

[39] If it doesn't, then this must be declared as an abstract class and one or more of its subclasses must implement any remaining unimplemented methods. I'll ignore this and say that any implementing class must contain the definitions of all methods that are named in the interface.

[40] Usually through shorthand's like `import java.lang.*` or `javax.swing.*`.

If you want to make your own named packages, there are some conventions and rules.

A package should only consist of a group of related classes–it is considered very wrong to put unrelated classes into a named package.

A package name has the form `ident.ident. … .ident`, where each component is a legal identifier. The first name should be the most general, then becoming more specific as you move right. For example, in `java.lang.String`, `java` is obviously very general, `lang` says that this will be a language support package, and `string` says that this is a collection of classes that manipulate `string` objects. Internally Java has a directory that contains, amongst other subdirectories, two subdirectories named `java` and `javax`. The `javax` directory will have a subdirectory called `lang`, which will have a subdirectory called `string`, which contains the `string` class.

To create a named package in a Java program that isn't in an integrated environment like BlueJ, NetBeans, or Eclipse, you put the command

```
package name
```

as the first line of your Java program, which has all of the classes that you want to be in your package, where `name` is any legitimate package name.

Now most Java programs are written in integrated environments, and they will have support to create packages. For example, in BlueJ the `Edit` tab pulldown includes the `New Package` control.

17.5 Exercises

General questions

1. In the sample interface class, salaries were rounded to an int as output, for example, $51667. Modify the output routines so that salaries will be output as, say, $33 or $1234 for salaries below $10,000, as, say, $12,345 for salaries with five or six digits, and as, say, $12,345,678 for salaries with seven or more digits. Assume that nobody has a salary at or above $1 billion.

2. Sometimes people get confused about the difference between inheritance and interfaces. Clearly explain why they are very different.

3. If the body of an interface class just contains one line, int fred(int n);, what does this mean? What constraints does it put on any class that implements the interface?

In-lab programs

1. Write a class named StringMethods that has no constructor or instance fields but has two methods. public static String[] breakString(String name) breaks up the name on spaces and returns an array containing the pieces. For example, if name contains "Susan M. Starkey" then the array will contain three values, "Susan", "M.", and "Starkey". public static String joinString(String[] pieces) joins the array elements into a String, separated by spaces. For example, joinString(breakString(name)) will always be name.

Out-lab programs

1. Write three classes Player, Batsman, and Bowler, as defined in Chapters 2 and 5.

2. Define an Interface class named IStringMethods that will let the above three classes use the methods defined in in-lab 1.

3. Modify the three classes so that they all have two methods getFullName() and getFirstName() that use the interface methods when needed.

Chapter 18. Exceptions and Exception Handling

18.1 Introduction

Unless you are either very lucky or very talented, occasionally you will have seen a bright red exception message in the bottom of your BlueJ output window when you have run your Java programs, which looked something like:

```
java.lang.ArrayIndexOutOfBoundsException: 3
        at Testit.main(Testit.java:13)
```

or

```
java.lang.StackOverflowError
        at Testit.factorial(Testit.java:11)
```

The first message says that it is throwing the `ArrayIndexOutOfBounds` exception because I've referred to element with subscript 3 of an array on line 13 of the `main` method in my `Testit`, and the array has three or less elements, and the second message says that I have blown out the stack, which probably means that I am in a recursive loop. So in both cases Java has detected a problem and has reacted to it by printing out this error message and quitting. Note that there are two different names for the types of object being thrown, the first is an exception and the second is an error. In this chapter I'll mainly be looking at exceptions, although I'll discuss errors at the end. Both exceptions and errors are in the `Throwable` class.

In Java when an exception handler finds a problem and prints a message like the first one it is called *throwing an exception*, but in the discipline the phrase *raising an exception* has historically been used more commonly. In this chapter I'll be looking at how to take control back when an exception is thrown, how the programmer can raise a system exception explicitly, and how to define and throw their own exceptions. Taking control back and handling a thrown exception is called *catching* the exception.

In this chapter I'll analyze solutions for a common problem and will use this as a way to describe how to catch system exceptions, independently throw and catch system exceptions, and throw and catch user-defined exceptions. The problem is how to make user input secure. Specifically, say that you have defined a `Scanner` named `in`, and ask the user to input a positive (> 0) `int` value. Assuming that `arrSize` is declared as an `int`, the insecure code to do this could be:

```
System.out.format("Please enter a positive int value:%n");
arrSize = in.nextInt();
```

Now if the user enters a value like 7 then you can continue without problems. However you should always assume that your users are either unintelligent or malicious, and that they'll get it wrong. So they might enter a value like 0 or -5, in which case you can already handle this by having code like

```
int arrSize;                // must be > 0
boolean badInput = true;    // used to repeat loop until valid input

while (badInput)
{
    System.out.format("Please enter a positive int value:%n");
    arrSize = in.nextInt();
    if (arrSize < 1)
        System.out.format("That was not positive. ");
    else
        valid = true;
}
```

And it will keep bullying the user until they finally get it right. However, users are usually much more creative than that. What if instead of an int they enter -3.4 or Denbigh? In both cases Java will raise its InputMismatchException, print out the exception message in red under BlueJ, and quit. One solution, which I'll go through in more detail throughout the rest of this chapter, is to use the code:

```
int arrSize = 0;            // must be > 0 when input
boolean badInput = true;    // used to repeat loop until valid input

while (badInput)
{
    try
    {
        System.out.format("Please enter a positive int value:%n");
        arrSize = in.nextInt();
        if (arrSize < 2)
            throw new MustBePositiveException();
        badInput = false;
    }
    catch (InputMismatchException exception)
    {
        String badValue = in.next();  // re-read bad value as a String
        System.out.format("Input must be an int, not %s, try again.%n",
                            badValue);
    }
    catch (MustBePositiveException exception)  // user defined exception
    {
        System.out.format("%d is not positive, try again.%n",
                            arrSize);
    }
}
```

There are some new concepts here, of which the most important are the try and catch blocks and the throw call. Describing what is going on here will take the rest of the chapter.

Java is one of a minority of programming languages that makes it easy for the programmer throw and catch exceptions, so in future you should make your

212

programs more secure by always using exception handling to protect your programs from their users. Without this users will quickly decide that they don't want to use your programs, because they will crash too often.

18.2 Standard Exceptions

Clicking on the `Exception` class in the Java 6 documentation you'll see that it has the following list of subclasses. Even though this looks a mess, it is actually worse because I've simplified things by removing the word `Exception` that is at the end of each of them, and so, for example, `AclNotFound` is actually `AclNotFoundException`.

```
AclNotFound, Activation, AlreadyBound, Application, AWT, BackingStore,
BadAttributeValueExp, BadBinaryOpValueExp, BadLocation,
BadStringOperation, BrokenBarrier, Certificate, ClassNotFound,
CloneNotSupported, DataFormat, DatatypeConfiguration, DestroyFailed,
Execution, ExpandVeto, FontFormat, GeneralSecurity, GSS, IllegalAccess,
IllegalClassFormat, Instantiation, Interrupted, Introspection,
InvalidApplication, InvalidMidiData, InvalidPreferencesFormat,
InvalidTargetObjectType, InvocationTarget, IO, JAXB, JM, KeySelector,
LastOwner, LineUnavailable, Marshal, MidiUnavailable, MimeTypeParse,
MimeTypeParse, Naming, NoninvertibleTransform, NoSuchField, NoSuchMethod,
NotBound, NotOwner, Parse, ParserConfiguration, Printer, Print,
PrivilegedAction, PropertyVeto, RefreshFailed, Remarshal, Runtime, SAX,
Script, ServerNotActive, SOAP, SQL, Timeout, TooManyListeners,
Transformer, Transform, UnmodifiableClass, UnsupportedAudioFile,
UnsupportedCallback, UnsupportedFlavor, UnsupportedLookAndFeel,
URIReference, URISyntax, User, XA, XMLParse, XMLSignature, XMLStream, and
XPath.
```

Many of these will have subclasses. The one that matters most for our needs is `RuntimeException`, which contains the following throwable exception names (again with `Exception` removed from the end of each one to make it easier to read).

```
AnnotationTypeMismatch, Arithmetic, ArrayStore, BufferOverflow,
BufferUnderflow, CannotRedo, CannotUndo, ClassCast, CMM,
ConcurrentModification, DOM, EmptyStack, EnumConstantNotPresent, Event,
IllegalArgument, IllegalMonitorState, IllegalPathState, IllegalState,
ImagingOp, IncompleteAnnotation, IndexOutOfBounds, JMRuntime, LS,
MalformedParameterizedType, MirroredType, MirroredTypes, MissingResource,
NegativeArraySize, NoSuchElement, NoSuchMechanism, NullPointer,
ProfileData, Provider, RasterFormat, RejectedExecution, Security, System,
TypeConstraint, TypeNotPresent, UndeclaredThrowable,
UnknownAnnotationValue, UnknownElement, UnknownType, UnmodifiableSet,
UnsupportedOperation, and WebService.
```

Some of these will also have subclasses defining yet more throwable exceptions. For example, `IndexOutOfBoundsException` has two subclasses, `ArrayIndexOutOfBoundsException` and `StringIndexOutOfBoundsException`, which includes the exception that I used as an example in the beginning of this chapter.

The reason that these lists are relevant is that Java lets you throw these exceptions yourself in your programs, as I'll show in Section 18.4, where you'll need to select one, probably from the RuntimeException list.

213

18.3 Catching Built-in Exceptions

I'll start with the most common situation, which is catching and handling an exception that has been thrown by the system. I'll simplify the example that I gave earlier and assume that the program is asking the user to enter any int value into a variable called newInt, and that it needs to be protected against the user putting in values like a double, String, or boolean. One way to do this is to use:

```
int newInt = 0;           // value will be reset by an input
boolean badInput = true;  // used to repeat loop until valid input

while (badInput)
{
    try
    {
        System.out.format("Please an int value:%n");
        newInt = in.nextInt();
        badInput = false;
    }
    catch (InputMismatchException exception)
    {
        String badValue = in.next();  // re-read bad value as a String
        System.out.format("Input must be an int, not %s, try again.%n",
        badValue);
    }
}
```

The while loop will just keep trying to get the user to enter an int value until they get it right. Once newInt = in.nextInt() succeeds without raising the exception, badInput will be set to false.

The try block contains three statements, and its meaning is to try executing these statements to see whether they succeed without raising an exception. Here the only way that an exception might be raised is if the user enters a value that isn't an int at the input line. If the user does enter an int value, then badInput is set to false, the catch block is ignored, and the program exits the while loop.

Things get more interesting when the user messes up and enters a value that isn't an int. At that point the system looks for an attached catch block that is catching the exception that has been raised. In this case Java will raise the exception called InputMismatchException and so its catch block will be executed. This will do the in.next() assignment and then output the error message to the user. It will then return control back to the end of the try block that called it (i.e., not the point where the exception was thrown). That is at the end of the while loop (it won't rerun the catch block a it is only called when its exception is raised), to that completes this run through the while loop. Since the statement resetting badInput has never been reached this causes the while loop to be repeated until the user enters an int value.

This leaves a couple of issues; how did I know that the exception that would be thrown was called `InputMismatchException` and what the `in.next()` statement is doing. The latter is a bit technical so I'll discuss that in Section 18.3.1, below.

As I showed earlier, there are a large number of possible exception names that Java could use. To find out which one will be used in any circumstance, so that you can catch it, first run your program without catching any exceptions, and behave like a malicious user and do your best to put in values (e.g., at input or when setting an array size) that will break the program. See what names Java uses as it raises exceptions and crashes your program and then catch these exceptions. So in this case I ran my program without the `catch` block, put in input values like aaa and `3.7`, found that both threw the `InputMismatchException` exception, so then added a `catch` for it.

18.3.1 Clearing Out the Bad Value in the Input Buffer after an Exception

The only remaining detail is the `in.next()` call in the `catch` block. Say that after you ask for an `int` the user enters a `String` like aaa or a `double` like `-3.5`. Java recognizes the error and raises the exception, and it then resets the input pointer to the front of the erroneous token so that it will also be the next value read. In this case I can use this feature by re-reading the bad input as a `String` using `in.next()`, and then including the bad value in the error message as I have in this `catch` block. Wit this a typical session could be:

```
Please enter a positive int
3.5
Input must be an int, not 3.5, try again.
Please enter a positive int
aaa
Input must be an int, not aaa, try again.
Please enter a positive int
7
```

and then execution will consider normally.

In other cases when you want to ignore the bad value you'll need to use in.nextLine(); to clear out the line that contains the bad value, because otherwise each in.nextInt() call will keep re-reading the same bad value without waiting for the user to enter a new value.

18.4 Explicitly Throwing a Built-in Exception

In the previous section I relied on the system throwing an exception if in.nextInt() attempted to read a token that wasn't an int. Sometimes you want your program to throw a built-in exception even if the system doesn't think that anything is wrong. As an example, I'll return to the problem that I introduced at the beginning of this cahapter, where I wanted the user to enter a positive int value. If the user entered an illegal int value (negative or zero) I first handled that by using an if-then-else statement, but it is often more convenient to use an exception.

One solution is:

```
int arrSize = 0;            // value will be reset by an input
boolean badInput = true;  // used to repeat loop until valid input

while (badInput)
{
    try
    {
        System.out.format("Please an int value:%n");
        newInt = in.nextInt();
        if (newInt > 0)
            badInput = false;
        else
            throw new InputMismatchException();
    }
    catch (InputMismatchException exception)
    {
        System.out.format("Input must be positive int, try again.%n");
        in.nextLine();
    }
}
```

Now if the user enters a zero or a negative number I'm explicitly raising the InputMismatchException exception at a time when Java wouldn't, because as far as it is concerned a value like -5 is a perfectly reasonable value for in.nextInt(). Note the format: the keyword throw, followed by new, followed by the exception name with parentheses at the end.

A problem with this is that the same exception is being raised for both a value that isn't an int and also for an int that isn't positive. This causes two problems; (a) I can't capture the bad value because in the first case it will still be available and in the second it has been successfully read, (b) I have to use the same error message for both situations, and (c) since I have no idea whether the input cursor is in front of or after the bad value I have to use in.nextLine() to clear out anything that remains on the input.

It would be better to throw a different exception for non-positive values.

The first decision to make is which built-in exception to throw. The problem will be at run time, so I'll limit myself to the subclasses of RuntimeException that I showed in Section 18.2. Look through the list before reading on and decide which is the most appropriate exception to throw for this problem. There are a few choices, but I've decided to useI think that IllegalArgument. Remember that its real name is IllegalArgumentException. This gives a modified version of my program:

```
int arrSize = 0;             // must be > 0 when input
boolean badInput = true;     // used to repeat loop until valid input

while (badInput)
{
    try
    {
        System.out.format("Please enter a positive int value:%n");
        arrSize = in.nextInt();
        if (arrSize < 2)
            throw new IllegalArgumentException();
        badInput = false;
    }
    catch (InputMismatchException exception)
    {
        String badValue = in.next();  // re-read bad value as a String
        System.out.format("Input must be an int, not %s, try again.%n",
                          badValue);
    }
    catch (IllegalArgumentException exception)
    {
        System.out.format("%d is not positive, try again.%n",
                          arrSize);
    }
}
```

This is slightly longer, but performs much better. By breaking the exceptions that I catch into two groups, a system thrown exception for non-integers and a user thrown exception tor non-positive integers I can output better error messages that include the bad values entered by the user.

One additional improvement that I could make would be to spend more time looking for a better exception to throw (i.e., a more appropriate name).

Many exceptions in RunTimeException have additional subclasses so I should check to see whether IllegalArgumentException has any. Click on it in the Java documentation and you'll find that it has a number, where I've removed the word Exception on the end of each subclass in the list below.

```
IllegalCharsetName, IllegalFormat, IllegalSelector, IllegalThreadState,
InvalidKey, InvalidOpenType, InvalidParameter, KeyAlreadyExists,
NumberFormat, PatternSyntax, UnresolvedAddress, UnsupportedAddressType,
and UnsupportedCharset.
```

```
None of these seem any better than IllegalArgumentException, so I'll
stick with that.
```

18.5 Rolling Your Own Exceptions

Java has so many exception classes that it is often easy to find one that you can raise when needed. However, if you want to create your own exception named, say, MustBePositiveException, then it is very easy to do in Java. There are a couple of reasons to do this; (a) you might prefer to name the exception yourself, rather than using one of the Jave exception names, and (b) if you choose a name like, say,

217

`IllegalArgumentException` to throw, then if that exception happens to be thrown independently by the system you'll catch it unexpectedly.

To create a new exception like this, which will be thrown at run time, all that I have to do is to make a new class that only contains:

```java
public class MustBePositiveException extends RuntimeException
{
    public MustBePositiveException()
    {
    }

    public MustBePositiveException(String message)
    {
        super(message);
    }
}
```

(Use this template for any other exceptions that you want to create, replacing the name `MustBePositive` with your exception name in all three places.) Then I can throw and catch this exception in my code replacing the exception name that I used in my last code sample, `IllegalArgumentException`, giving the code that I first showed in Section 18.1. It is so trivial to do create new exception names like this in Java that you might as well do it in most cases where you want to throw an exception. Obviously this can only be used for the user throwing an exception, not the system throwing an exception.

18.6 Summary of Exception Handling

There are a few simple rules for exception handling in Java:

Put any dangerous code (i.e., where exceptions might be thrown) into a try block. Run your program without any catch blocks and try to behave like a creative and malicious user. That is, put in any values that you suspect could break your program and write down the names of any exceptions that get thrown by the system. Add catch blocks to handle all of these exceptions.
If you want to throw an exception, system or user-defined, use the statement throw new ExceptionName();
If the code in the tryblock executes without an exception being thrown (which you expect will happen nearly all of the time), the catch block(s) will be ignored and control will be passed to the statement, or }, after the end of the last attached catch block.
If an exception is thrown, control is passed to the appropriate catch block, its code is executes, and then control is passedto the statement, or }, that follows the end of the last attached catch block. If no catch block has the name of the exception, the program terminates.
To define a user-defined exception, use the template shown in Section 18.5.

18.7 Exceptions *vs.* Errors

If you look at the Java 6 docs, you'll find that the `Throwable` class has two subclasses, `Exception` and `Error`. In general it is a good programming for your Java program to catch any `Exception` that might occur, but it is not usually expected that you will provide handlers for thrown `Error` conditions. The direct subclasses of the `Error` class are:

```
AnnotationFormatError, AssertionError, AWTError, CoderMalfunctionError,
FactoryConfigurationError, FactoryConfigurationError, IOError,
LinkageError, ServiceConfigurationError, ThreadDeath,
TransformerFactoryConfigurationError, and VirtualMachineError.
```

and it should be fairly obvious that most of these are beyond user control.

18.8 Exercises

General questions

1. If you were to throw an exception whenever the `batAvg()` method in the `Player` class in Chapter 1 was called with atBats containing zero, which built-in exception would you use?

2. If you were to throw an exception whenever the constructor method in the `Player` class in Chapter 1 was called with more hits than atBats, which built-in exception would you use?

3. Say a method contains the statement `x = y / z;` where x, y, and z are all integers. If z is zero Java throws the exception `ArithmeticException` when this statement is executed. Show how to protect this statement by catching the exception and by setting x to `Integer.MAX_VALUE` (which is the largest possible integer value) when the exception is thrown.

4. If Java throws an exception when a `Scanner` input is entered because the type is wrong (e.g., the user enters a `String` value when a `double` was expected) and the program catches the exception, it resets the input pointer back to the beginning of the problem input. Why does it do this?

5. When I originally introduced exceptions I said that the most important high-level exception was `RunTimeException`. Why did I claim this?

6. Consider the following code segment. Why will it loop if a value is entered that isn't a `double`?

```
int newValue;
boolean badInput = true;   // used to repeat loop until valid input

while (badInput)
{
    try
    {
        System.out.format("Please enter a double value:%n");
        newValue = in.nextDouble();
        badInput = false;
    }
    catch (InputMismatchException exception)
    {
        System.out.format("Input must be an int, try again.%n");
    }
}
```

In-lab programs

1. In Chapter 2 I introduced my first class, which had a single method, `batAvg()`, which divided `hits` (cast to a double) by `atBats`. Fix that class so that it is more stable. Specifically have three user-defined exceptions that are thrown if the number of hits is greater than the number of at bats in the constructor, if `atBats` is zero when `batAvg()` is called, or if the number of hits is negative. Catch these exceptions, as well as the potential divide by zero exception in batAvg(), and perform reasonable actions that let execution continue.

Out-lab programs

1. Modify the program in in-lab 1 by using Scanner input for all values when creating an object. Make the program user-proof by throwing and catching exceptions for everything that you can consider a malicious user doing to break your program. For example, they will probably attempt to enter a `double` or a `String` each time that you expect an `int` input, for values like the number of hits. As usual, assume that your user is stupid, vindictive, or both, and will rarely follow instructions.

Chapter 19. Reading from and Writing to External Files

19.1 Introduction

In all of your programs so far you have been reading from the standard input and writing to the standard output. Obviously for most applications this isn't an appropriate approach. For example, if I want to write a Java program that finds out how many times the word Denmark appears in *Hamlet*, I don't want to have to type the whole play in as input, but would much prefer to find a file somewhere that contains the text of *Hamlet* and then read in lines from the file looking for the word Denmark. Or it would be nice, when computing grades from a spreadsheet, if I could just write out a file containing student names, IDs, and final grades and send them directly to the Registrar's Office.

Reading from and writing to external files is pretty easy in Java and in fact you've already seen most of the features with the I/O statements that you've been using. So I'll demonstrate external files with two simple programs, one just for input from an external file and one also for output to an external file.

19.2 Reading from a File

This uses the `Scanner` class that I've been using with the default `System.in` file, which is the standard input, but applied to a named file on your computer. So previously I've been using:

```
Scanner in = new Scanner(System.in);
```

and now I'll use

```
Scanner infile = new Scanner(fileHandle);
```

where `fileHandle` refers to a specific file on your computer. So first we have to specify what that file is, which is done by instancing the `FileReader` class with the command:

```
FileReader fileHandle = new FileReader("actual file name");
```

For example, if I want to read from the file `/Users/starkey/cs160/demo.txt` on my Mac, I would use the two declarations:

```
FileReader demoHandle = new FileReader("/Users/starkey/cs160/demo.txt");
Scanner infile = new Scanner(demoHandle);
```

and then I can use all of the usual `Scanner` methods like `next()` and `next.Double()` to get values out of the file.

On a Windows system the first line could be:

```
FileReader demoHandle = new FileReader("C:\cs160\demo.txt");
```

19.3 Some Overhead Details

`FileReader` is in `java.io.FileReader` and as we have seen before `Scanner` is in `java.util.Scanner`, so I'll need to import both `java.io.*` and `java.util.*`.

A bigger hassle is that Java knows that file reads and writes often fail, either because the file doesn't exist or because you don't have appropriate access permissions to the file. As a result Java requires that any program that reads or writes to an external file must catch the exception `FileNotFoundException`. So the I/O component must always be in a `try` block that is followed by a `catch` block.

19.4 A File Input Example

Now I'll demo this with a short piece of code in the main method. The program will read all the tokens (words) from a file and print them out on separate lines. For example, if I run the program when the external file contains

```
Denbigh Starkey was
born in England.

The town of Denbigh
is in North Wales.
```

I want the output shown below:

```
Denbigh
Starkey
was
born
in
England.
The
town
of
Denbigh
is
in
North
Wales.
```

The program is:

```java
import java.util.*;   // to use Scanner
import java.io.*;     // to use FileReader
public class FileHandler
{
    public static void main()
    {
        final String filename = "/users/starkey/cs160/demo.txt";

        try
        {
            FileReader infile = new FileReader(filename);
            Scanner in = new Scanner(infile);
            String next;  // reads in the next token

            while (in.hasNext())
            {
                next = in.next();
                System.out.println(next);
            }

            in.close();
        }
        catch (FileNotFoundException exception)
        {
            System.out.format("Cannot open %s for reading",
                              filename);
        }
    }
}
```

The major new feature here is the FileReader class, which, as discussed above, sets infile up as the file handle of the input file. A file handle object is just the name of the file that is used in the program.

The program has the required try and catch blocks, as discussed earlier. The catch does nothing sophisticated but just prints out a message saying that the file could not be opened.

The hasNext() method returns true if there is at least one more token available for reading and false if the scanner has reached the end of the file. Many programming languages handle this differently and return EOF as the last read, which can then be tested in a loop, but Java's approach is probably nicer. Look at the Scanner methods in the Java 6 docs for all of the has.Something() methods.

19.5 Reading from Files and Writing to Files

I'll again use an example to demonstrate this. The program will read from an external file and write any line that contains the string Denbigh to a new external file. So if, for example, the input file contains the lines used for the previous program, then the output file will contain

```
Denbigh Starkey was
The town of Denbigh
```

after the program executes. I'll show the code first, in a `main()`, and will then discuss it.

```java
public static void main()
{
    final String infilename = "/Users/starkey/cs160/demo.txt",
                 outfilename = "/Users/starkey/cs160/demo.out",
                 search = "Denbigh";
    boolean badin = true;

    try
    {
        FileReader infile = new FileReader(infilename);
        Scanner in = new Scanner(infile);
        badin = false;  // infile read succeeded

        PrintWriter outfile = new PrintWriter(outfilename);
        String next;  // next input line

        while (in.hasNextLine())
        {
            next = in.nextLine();
            if (next.indexOf(search) >= 0)
                outfile.println(next);
        }

        in.close();
        outfile.close();
    }

    catch (FileNotFoundException exception)
    {
        if (badin)  // Input file open failed
            System.out.format("Cannot open %s for reading%n",infilename);
        else        // Output file open failed
            System.out.format("Cannot open %s for writing%n",outfilename);
    }
}
```

I've put the file names and search string (Denbigh) at the top of the method so that it is easy for a user to run the program with a different search string and different files. I could also have read these three values in as user input. Once set, the file names and search string shouldn't be changed, so I've declared them all as final.

The boolean named badin is used when a FileNotFoundException is thrown to tell whether it was the input or the output file access that failed. Since it is set in the try block and used in the catch block, it must be declared outside both blocks. I initialize it to true and then reset it to false once the input file open succeeds. The catch uses this to print out useful messages like:

```
Cannot open /Users/starkey/cs160/demo.out for writing
```

We saw the use of FileReader and how to set up a Scanner object for it in the last section of this chapter. Here a new PrintWriter object named outfile is set up for output, and once we have it, we can use all of the usual output methods like print(), println(), and format(). Here I only need to use println() when I use outfile.println(next). So if you want something to go to standard output, then

224

you use `System.out.method()` and you can directly replace this with `outfile.method()` to get the same values written to `outfile`.

It is always a good idea to close any file that you've opened, which I do at the end.

In the previous program I used `in.hasNext()` to determine whether there were any tokens left in the input file. Here I've used `in.hasNextLine()` to see whether there are any remaining lines left. For this program it won't matter which I use, but if, say, I were counting lines in the input file and the last line only contained spaces, then using `hasNextLine()` would be necessary because `in.hasNext()` would quit before counting the last line.

Finally, there is the code that looks for lines that contain `Denbigh`. The `indexOf()` method looks for the argument in the string object. If it is there, it returns the character index of the beginning of the first occurrence, where the first character in the string has index 0. If the potential substring does not appear in the string, then `indexOf()` will return -1.

For example:

```
String str = "Denbigh";
System.out.println(str.indexOf("ig"));
System.out.println(str.indexOf("gi"));
```

would output

```
4
-1
```

So in this program the code

```
if (next.indexOf(search) >= 0)
    outfile.println(next);
```

is testing whether the string `search` is a substring of the string `next`.

19.6 Exercises

General questions

1. I have a program that includes:

```
final String infilename = "/Users/starkey/cs160/demo.txt",
             outfilename = "/Users/starkey/cs160/demo.out";
```

and later contains the lines:

```
FileReader infile = new FileReader(infilename);
PrintWriter outfile = new PrintWriter(outfilename);
```

Assume that demo.txt is a file that just contains int values, and that it contains at least one value. Give the Java code to read the first value from the file demo.txt and then write it to the file demo.out.

2. Java requires that all programs that use external files must catch FileNotFoundException. Argue for or against this decision.

In-lab programs

1. Write a method that opens a file of words for reading and outputs the number of characters in the file, the number of words in the file, and the number of lines in the file.

2. Write a method that reads words from a text file and outputs them, one word per line, in reverse order from the way that they were in the text file. Do this by putting them into an array list.

Out-lab programs

1. Write a method whose parameter is a file name which it opens for reading and creates a 1D array of objects of type stringNum, which is a class that you write that contains two intance fields, a String and an int. The array will contain unique tokens from the file and the number of times that it appears. E.g., if an entry in the array contains the string Susan and the int 5 then this means that the token Susan appears five times in the file.

2. Add a method to your class in Question 1, above, that sorts the file lexicographically (look at the compare() method in the string class) and outputs the pairs in order.

Appendix A: Downloading BlueJ and the Java JDK

In this book I've used BlueJ, which is an integrated development environment (IDE) which makes it easier to develop and debug Java programs. If you expect to just use the computers in your university's PC labs, then Java and BlueJ are probably installed on them. If, however, you will be using your own computer then the first thing that you'll need to do is to download and install both systems.

If you continue to program in Java, you'll probably move later to a more complex IDE than BlueJ, like Eclipse or NetBeans, which can also be downloaded free, but those systems are far more complex than BlueJ, and have a much steeper learning curve. By comparison BlueJ provides what you need at this time, and won't distract you from the process of learning to program.

A.1 Installing BlueJ

This is usually vary easy, so I will look at it first. There are three versions of BlueJ available, for the Mac, for Windows systems, and for other systems like Linux.

Go to www.bluej.org, download the version for your operating system, click on it to uncompress it if needed, and do the obvious things like moving it into the appropriate folder (e.g., the Applications folder if you are on a Mac). You should be able to install it on any standard system in just a few minutes.

A.1 Installing the Java JDK

You need Java, which is used by BlueJ, but it must be the Java Development Kit (JDK) not just the Java Runtime Environment (JRE). So before doing anything else, check to see whether you have Java on your system–if you don't then you'll need to install it. The easiest way to check is to try running BlueJ and see whether it works, or whether it says that you still need the JDK.

If you have a Mac, the JDK will be already installed unless you are using an ancient version of the OS that is older than OS X. So assuming that you're running Leopard or Snow Leopard then installation is not needed since you should already have all of the appropriate Java files already installed.

If you are running under a Windows system you should install JDK 6 or JDK 7, from http://java.sun.com/javase/downloads/index.jsp.

Index

!

! · 105

{

{} · 13

*

*/ · 25
*= · 66

/

/* · 25
/** · 25
/= · 66

&

&& · 105

%

%= · 66

+

+= · 66

=

-= · 66

|

| | · 105

3

3D array · 171

A

abstract method · 206
access specifier · 13
accessor · 70
actual parameter · 15, 31
actual parameters · 30
add() · 154
Algol 60 · 2
algorithm · 2
and · 105
Animation · 8
args · 33
arithmetic exception · 44
array · 143
array list · 143, 153
array parameter · 168
ArrayList class · 153
Artificial Intelligence · 8
assembler · 7
assembly language · 7
assignment statement · 15
autoboxing · 159

B

barber pole (BlueJ) · 43
base case · See recursion
Best Jobs in America · 8
binary digit · 5
bit · 5
block of code · 13
BlueJ · xi, 23
boolean · 51, 159
boxing · 159

breakpoint · 133
byte · 5, 50, 159
bytecode · 7

C

cache memory · 6
cast · 17
casting functions · 65
Central Processing Unit · *See* CPU
char · 51
Character · 159
class field · 78
class name · 13
class variable · 78
class. · 11
clear() · 154
clock cycle · 4
cohesion · 197
cohesive · 197
command line arguments · 33
comment · 14, 25
commenting variable declarations · 48
comparison operators · 95
compile button (BlueJ) · 26
compile error · 7, 41
compiler · 4, 7
Computer Architecture · 8
Computer Science · 8
conditional · 93
constant · 102
constructor · 12
Constructor Definition · 15
constructor name · 15
correctness · 1
Coupling · 79
CPU · 4

D

Data Mining · 8
Databases · 8
Deakin University · xii
debugger · 44, 45, 133
declaring variables · 47
dialog box · 119
dialog boxes · 29
directory (BlueJ) · 23
divide · 17
documentation · 83
double · 17, 50, 159
do-while · 128, 131
dynamic · 153

E

Eclipse · xi
efficiency · 1
else-if · 98
encapsulation · 18
exception · 211
execute · 4
execution error · 43
execution errors · 7
external file · 221
external files · 29

F

factorial · 177
file · 221
file handle · 221, 223
file I/O · 29
FileReader · 222
float · 50, 159
floating point · 17, 50
for statement · 127, 128
foreach · 132, 149
formal parameter · 15
formatted output · 29
free format · 14

G

Game Development · 8
GB · *See* gigabyte
GHz · 4
gigabyte · 6
Graphics · 8

H

high coupling · 80
homogeneous · 143, 153

I

IDE · xi
identifier · 48
identifier name · 49
identifying objects · 11
if · 93
if-then-else · 96
immutable · 70
implements · 203

implicit parameter, · 31
infinite loop · 43
inheritance · 11
initial value · 47
initializing an array · 148
instance · 12
instance field · 12, 13, 78
instance variable · 12
`int` · 17, 49
Integer · 159
integer divide · 65
interface · 201
interface class · 201, 202
internal clock · 4
interpreter · 7

J

Java Development Kit · 23, 227
Java Runtime Environment · 227
Javadoc · 83, 89
JDK · 23, 227
JOptionPane · 119
JRE · 227
JUnit · 33

K

K · *See* kilobyte
KB · *See* kilobyte
kilobyte · 6
Knuth, Don · 6

L

left justified output · 114
length (array) · 145
long · 50, 159
loop control condition · 129
loop statements · 125
loop, recursive · 182
low coupling · 80

M

machine language · 7
main() · 32
Mars Climate Orbiter · 1
Mars Polar Lander · 1
MB · *See* megabyte
mebibyte · 6
megabyte · 6

memory · 5
    cache · 6
method · 12
method declaration · 16
MiB · 6
Money Magazine · 8
mutator · 70

N

nanosecond · 5
nested loop · 165
NetBeans · xi
Networking · 8
non-rectangular array · 170
not · 105
NP-Complete · 8
numeric types · 50

O

object · 11, 12
object-oriented design · 2
object-oriented language · 2, 11
object-oriented programming · 2
objects first · xi
OOD · *See* object-oriented design
OOL · *See* object-oriented language
OOP · *See* object-oriented programming
Operating Systems · 8
or · 105
output buffer · 32
output window (BlueJ) · 31

P

packages · 207
polymorphism · 202
Precedence of **boolean** Operators · 106
Primitive Data Types · 49
print() · 30
println() · 30
private · 13
processor · *See* CPU
program · 2
programming · 1
Programming Language Design · 8
project name · 23
protected · 13
public · 13

R

raising an exception · 43
RAM · *See* random access memory
random access memory · 5
recursion · 177
recursive loop · 182
recursive method · 177
remove() · 154
right justified output · 114
run · 4

S

Scanner · 221
scope of variables · 52
selection · 104
short · 50, 159
short circuit · 106
Simulation · 8
single step · 133
size() · 154
Software Engineer · 8
software engineering · 4
Software Security · 8
StackOverflowError · 183
static · 78, 143
static field · 78
static variable · 78
subscript · 145
Sun Microsystems · xii
Swing · 119
switch · 99
System · 30
System.out.format() · 30
System.out.print() · 29

System.out.println() · 29, 31

T

TB · *See* terabyte
terabyte · 6
Theory of Computer Science · 8
Therac-25 · 1
this · 16, 53
throwing an exception · 43
token · 119
tolerance · 36
Tower of Hanoi · 178
truth table · 105
type casting · 65

U

unboxing · 159
unit test · 33
University of Kent · xii

V

variable · 47
Visualization · 8
volatile · 6

W

while loop · 126, 130
wrapper class · 159